"Irving Oyle does it again, even in a bigger way—of course, he has the support of his partner, Susan Jean. I was enthralled with their writing from word one. *The Wizdom Within* clearly and simply inspires and guides us on how to use our greatest healing tool—our doctor within. This is the ultimate self-help book."
— Elson M. Haas, M.D.,
Author of *Staying Healthy With Nutrition*
and *Staying Healthy With the Seasons*

"Nobody makes ancient wisdom more contemporary and accessible than Irving Oyle and Susan Jean. Besides that, their lighthearted yet well-reasoned approach is fun—and it can change your life as quickly as you can change your mind."
— Martin L. Rossman, M.D.,
Author of *Healing Yourself: A Step-by-Step*
Program for Better Health Through Imagery

"A most important book that is easy to read, filled with wit, practical examples, and exercises, and certain to uplift your spirit and your life."
— Gerald G. Jampolsky, M.D.,
Author of *Love Is Letting Go of Fear*

"Dr. Irving Oyle and Susan Jean have written a highly readable guide to making your dreams come true. Their easy, accessible methods of daydreaming your way into the life you want is backed by inspiring personal stories of their clients and by scientific evidence emerging from the new physics. Their infectious humor and enthusiasm make this an engaging and empowering book."
— John Broomfield, Ph.D.,
Author of *Other Ways of Knowing*,
and Jo Imlay, M.J.

Other Books
by Dr. Irving Oyle

The Healing Mind
Magic, Mysticism, and Modern Medicine
The New American Medicine Show
Time, Space and the Mind

THE **WIZ**DOM WITHIN

On Daydreams,
Realities,
and Revelations

*Dr. Irving Oyle
and
Susan Jean*

H J KRAMER INC
Tiburon, California

Published by H J Kramer Inc
P.O. Box 1082
Tiburon, CA 94920

Editor: Nancy Grimley Carleton
Cover Design: Spectra Media
Composition: Classic Typography
Book Production: Schuettge & Carleton
Manufactured in the United States of America
10 9 8 7 6 5 4 3 2 1

Library of Congress Cataloging-in-Publication Data

Oyle, Irving. 1925–
    The wizdom within : on daydreams, realities, and revelations / by
Irving Oyle and Susan Jean.
    p. cm.
    ISBN 0–915811–42–1 : $11.95
    1. Self-realization. 2. Mental suggestion. 3. Therapeutics,
Suggestive. 4. Medicine and psychology. I. Jean, Susan.
II. Title. III. Title: Wisdom within.
BF637.S4096 1992
158—dc20   92–53162
                                                                  CIP

To life, liberty,
and the pursuit of happiness.

*Many of
the tales we
tell in this book are
composite case histories
from the files of the
Transformational
Learning
Center.*

Susan Jean and Dr. Irving Oyle

To Our Readers
The books we publish
are our contribution to
an emerging world based on
cooperation rather than on competition,
on affirmation of the human spirit rather
than on self-doubt, and on the certainty
that all humanity is connected.
Our goal is to touch as many
lives as possible with a
message of hope for
a better world.

Hal and Linda Kramer,
Publishers

Contents

Acknowledgments

We'd like to acknowledge Carl Jung, Albert Schweitzer, Hans Selye, Albert Einstein, Karl Pribram, Dean Ornish, James Lovelock, our editor Nancy Grimley Carleton, all our clients and their allies, our Shih Tzu dogs, Himalayan cats, and assorted birds and plants. Their teachings form the basis for this book and our lives.

Introduction

We're all brilliant. We're all surrounded by abundance. We all have things that go right for us every day. It's just that sometimes we don't notice.

This book is about de-hypnotizing yourself so that you can enjoy today. It's about getting to know yourself better. It's about figuring out what you love to do and doing it—for your health, happiness, and peace of mind.

As you will see by reading this book, we each have our own expert answers and positive solutions within ourselves. Everyone knows how to daydream. We will show you how to tap into your own infinite, innate wisdom by daydreaming . . . practical daydreaming.

We've worked with thousands of clients over the years. The method we've perfected through these experiences we present to you here. It has proven to be successful, enjoyable, and simple beyond our expectations. Our clients get their own valid, illuminating answers, time after time. We are all capable of improving our coping skills with this inner life-guidance system.

We suggest that you read through all the chapters once to get the general ideas. Then, if you like, give yourself a week or so to let the information settle in, read it again, and actually do the exercises and visualizations. From then on, focus on applying this method in your daily life for symptom relief, problem solving, and creating a new personal reality. We have yet to find the limits of its potential.

After you've studied the material presented here, you may want more information or guidance in applying it to your individual situation. If that is the case, we encourage you to give us a call. We can help you by telephone. Check the end of the book for our phone numbers.

Now, sit back and enjoy watching your perceptions being rearranged and your world transformed!

1

Free Fall

Wonder after wonder,
the universe unfolds.
LAO-TZU

"Every time I washed the car, it rained. It was uncanny. If I was going up, the next elevator was sure to be a downer. That was the story of my life before the accident."

Benny was a born-again Buddhist from India. He and I, Irving, met in Mendocino. At the time, I was newly divorced and wondering what to do with the rest of my life. We were sitting on a log on the beach and he was telling me about his transformation.

"Before the accident," he said, "I was a practicing diabetic shooting forty units of insulin a day and living alone. One sunny afternoon, I decided to go for a drive in the country instead of washing the car. Pretty soon, I was on a one-lane bridge doing about thirty-five miles per hour and saw a pickup truck coming from the other direction, doing about the same. There was no way either of us could stop in time to avoid a head-on collision, so I figured this was it. The end. I just closed my eyes and waited for it to happen. To tell you the truth, I wasn't even scared. Just relieved.

"The next thing I knew, I was on the other side of the bridge, off the road, in a shallow ditch. I turned off the engine, got out of the car, and looked back. No way

1

two vehicles could have passed each other in that space, yet there was no sign of a collision. Everything looked perfectly normal. It was really weird. Then I noticed the silence. Absolute, total silence. Not even a bird sound. So I figured I was dead and in Bardo."

He turned to me and explained, "Bardo, according to Tibetan Buddhism, is the state of consciousness between death and rebirth. It's when people look at lessons learned in the last life and program the next one. As I looked back, I realized that I had learned about self-fulfilling prophecies. So I decided that this time around, I was going to see things differently. No more Murphy's law for me. I closed my eyes and saw myself in a new life, totally healthy, happily married, and extremely lucky. I could actually feel the joy and contentment. Then, I got back into the car, eased it out of the ditch, and drove back into the world of appearances. The place you Westerners call the real world."

"And?" I asked.

"So far, so good. Three months after the accident, I can control my blood sugar without insulin, I met and have married a wonderful woman who loves to cook and owns her own home, and, as my English teacher used to say, everything keeps coming up roses.

"Looks like there's a storm coming in. I had better be on my way. Nice meeting you."

For a while, I just sat there, watching my thoughts. Where I see reality, Benny sees appearances. That could explain the phantom pickup truck. Maybe to him, it was just another appearance—an illusion. Of course! That's what it was—a hallucination triggered by an insulin reaction. Benny probably forgot to eat after he took his shot. But what about the transformation from a life of insulin shots and despair to a life of love and happiness? Sure seems like he really did that.

❀   ❀   ❀

December 21st: the shortest day of the year. Outside, a winter storm. Howling wind, driving rain, bitter cold, and pitch black. The end of the world. Indoors, warm and dry. Crackling fire in the wood stove, soft music on the stereo, frozen dinner in the microwave. Suddenly, the lights go out. The rain stops and the wind dies. Maybe I do, too. In this pitch black utter silence, it sure feels like it.

Like Jonah in the belly of the whale, I light a candle and look around at where I am. In the birth canal, between existences. Old life over, new one nowhere in sight. So how do I get from here to there? Free fall. Just relax and watch nature take its course. A bit of Benny's Bardo-type programming can't hurt. Maybe I can consciously set the scene for my next go-round in the world of appearances. What you see is what you get. Can't see myself living alone. Might as well program a relationship with a bright, attractive woman who has a sense of humor and a knack for cooking. I can see her saying she likes me and inviting me to come home with her and be her friend. We can work together and live in Hawaii. I feel myself getting warmer already. I think I might read a while by candlelight. I grab a book and flip it open.

3

The book turns out to be *Walden* by Thoreau. The passage that catches my eye goes something like this: "If a man moves confidently in the direction of his dreams and endeavors to live the life he has imagined, he will meet with success unexpected in common hours and begin to live with the license of a higher order of being." With this encouragement, and remembering Benny's success story, I fall asleep making images of my new life.

Next morning, in my mailbox, I find an airline ticket to Kona, Hawaii. A magical materialization? Mere coincidence? A scene in a very vivid dream? Probably all of the above. There is a cover letter in the envelope addressed to me. A minister who has read another of my books, *The Healing Mind*, is inviting me to fly over and speak to his congregation. Maybe do a seminar.

"We'll pay all your expenses, put you up at the Hilton, and reimburse you for your time. I know what the weather is like in your neck of the woods this time of the year, so I include the enclosed airline ticket, hoping it will constitute an offer you can't refuse."

He is right. I can't.

At about the same time, in Kona, on the big island of Hawaii, a young woman executive is terminating a dead-end relationship. The affair has no future because the guy is already married. For her, this is phase two of a three-stage plan she has devised to take charge of her life and make something of it. Phase one, resigning a demanding position that left no time for fun, is already complete. She ended that on the same positive note she is ending the relationship.

Susan can tell you more about it: "I made a special dinner for him one night and told him that I loved him very, very much. That I always had, and that I always would. I told him I was grateful for all he had taught me, but it was time for me to move on. I made sure he was okay. I made sure he knew it was absolutely nothing he had said or done. It was just that I was ready to get married. For the first time in my life, I was ending a relationship with unconditional love and clear communication. Then I made a little affirmation card on which I wrote down the characteristics that I would like to have in a husband. I think it said, 'I love and am loved by a man who is . . .' Some of the descriptive words I used were *kind, funny, intelligent, easygoing*. I wrote that down, stuck it in a book, and forgot about it. Three months later, I met him. As far as I'm concerned, I drew him to me in Hawaii all the way from Mendocino, California, thus completing phase three of my plan to begin living the life I had dreamed."

The kind of life we lead depends less on the goals we set for ourselves than it does on how we go about achieving them. "Hunting" for a husband or a wife, for instance, is not the same as creating a mate. The "hunt" usually involves singles' bars, computer dating services, and lots of goal-directed socializing.

The homebody in Susan, the part that loves animals, cooking, simplicity, solitude, peace, and quiet, isn't about to travel down that path. This would be just another version of the workaholic life-style she has decided isn't worthwhile. Raising and breeding pedigreed cats has taught her that if you want to catch an animal, hot pursuit is the worst possible approach. So when she reads that you can create a mate by listing the characteristics you'd like him or her to have, and then acting as if it were an accomplished fact, she decides it is worth a try. After following these instructions, Susan puts the matter out of her mind and goes back to living one day at a time. It isn't long before a local minister in Kona asks if she would help him organize a church retreat. Susan has never been on a retreat, church or otherwise. But, since the minister is a friend of a friend and the featured speaker sounds as if his teachings might aid her in her plan to improve the quality of her life, she agrees.

When I, Irving, step off the plane in Honolulu, my life is pretty empty. All I have are two suitcases, the clothes on my back, and a license to practice medicine. I don't even have a permanent place to live. But I know that nature hates a vacuum and tends to fill what's empty, so that is okay. Not knowing what to do next, I just stand there, waiting for instructions.

"DOCTOR OYLE. DOCTOR IRVING OYLE. PICK UP A WHITE COURTESY TELEPHONE, PLEASE."

I find the phone, pick it up, and tell it my name. It thanks me and instructs me to proceed to the building exit opposite baggage carousel number 42. Once outside, I am to look for a white Thunderbird with a woman driver. Carrying my two suitcases, following the white courtesy telephone's instructions, I feel like a kid on a magical mystery tour. For most kids, I guess, that's what life is. It is for us grown-ups, too—if we take the time to notice.

Lucille and her new car, Simonton Worthington T-Bird, are waiting at the curb. A school principal married to a banker, she was a member of Reverend Jerry's church in Kona before moving to Honolulu. He has asked her to pick me up at the airport and book me into a hotel because it is too late to catch the last interisland flight for Kona. On the way into town, she wants to know if I am planning to go home right after the retreat or if I am thinking about spending some time in the islands. I say that as of now, for me, Hawaii is home and, for the second time in six weeks, I get an offer I can't refuse. Lucille asks if I have a place to live.

"For tonight," I tell her, "I'll be living at the hotel you're taking me to. For the next week, I understand there's a place for me at the retreat grounds on the big island of Hawaii. After that, I'm sure something else will turn up. It always does."

Lucille giggles and says that maybe it already has. She tells me that she and her husband are set to start a two-month tour of Australia starting tomorrow. "About a week ago, the lady who was supposed to house-sit for us said she couldn't do it. Unexpected business on the mainland. That really put us in a bind. We can't just take off and leave the place empty. I'd spend my whole vacation worrying about what might be happening to it. That would ruin everything. For the past seven days, we've been making phone calls, repeating affirmations, and hoping for a miracle. We finally decided, if we don't

7

get someone by bedtime tonight, the trip is off. Could I talk you into staying at our house for a couple of months? It's quite comfortable and has its own beach. You wouldn't have to do anything. Just occupy it. I can relax and have a good time if I know someone trustworthy is living in it. We've already arranged to keep everything in working order. Telephone, cable TV, trash pickup, pool maintenance, and the housekeeper, who comes in once a week to do laundry and tidy up. You can use Simon to get around in. He's a bit of a gas guzzler, but he is reliable and always gets you where you want to go. I think you'll find the place quite comfortable, and you would be doing us a great service."

"Okay," I say. "Glad to help out."

Lucille heaves a huge sigh of relief. "That was a close one. Right down to the wire. It did teach me something, though. Now I know what Ken Keyes means when he talks about raising your addictions to preferences. Before I could go on this trip, I had to be willing to give it up."

After checking me in at the hotel, Lucille gives me an address, a house key, a set of car keys, a peck on the cheek, and drives off happy as a clam. Before leaving, she tells me, "A psychologist from the university is giving a talk on kahuna tradition at the hotel this evening. Check it out. I think you'll find it interesting."

When the room is full, a tallish woman with graying hair saunters in pulling a length of chain. She pulls it up to the podium, turns to face the audience, and asks, "Are there any questions up to this point?" Naturally, someone wants to know why she is pulling a chain.

Holding it up, she asks, "Did you ever try pushing one of these things?"

When the room gets quiet again, she goes on. "Chances are you have. And still do. A chain just like this one except that it's invisible. We forge it with our minds. I'm talking about the chain of cause and effect. Whenever you're working at trying to see if you can make something happen, you are pushing it. This chain illustrates a particular view of our world and how it works. Wouldn't it be easier and more effective to guide it rather than trying to push it with a combination of dogged determination, brute force, and hard work?"

Then she quotes the passage from Thoreau that struck me during the storm back in Mendocino—the one about moving confidently in the direction of your dreams and living as though they were already realized. She says this is in line with the kahuna teaching that dreams and other visions are seeds. Stating the theory in contemporary psychological terms, we could say that a daydream is a seed that when implanted in the unconscious mind and nurtured with confidence initiates a flow of events that carry it to fruition in time-space reality. ("What you see is what you get!" I think.) Notice that I said "flow of events" rather than "chain of events." The speaker continues, "Kahuna tradition sees the natural world as a manifestation of mana, the water of life. So if you know about water, you know about life. Water likes to flow along the line of least resistance. Try grabbing it and it runs through your fingers. Cup your hands to create an empty space, get in the flow, and presto!

your cup runneth over. From this point of view, it makes no more sense to think of life as a random assortment of isolated, independent objects and events than it does to see a river as a collection of isolated, independent drops of water."

Then she begins talking about Parsifal, a wet-behind-the-ears kid who lived in the Middle Ages and wanted to become a knight in King Arthur's court. On his way to Camelot, he wandered into a country that was a total wasteland. Nothing would grow, animals couldn't reproduce, and people walked around like zombies.

Someone took him to see the king, whose name was Amfortas. The king was in bed with a gaping wound in his groin. The wound was so terrible, legend has it, that he kept it on a pillow beside the bed. Without knowing why, Parsifal sensed that the wound had something to do with the desolate state the country was in. Someone asked if he had any idea what might help it heal, and two questions popped into his mind. He decided they were dumb questions so he said no and went on his way.

He wandered in a huge circle and, after a while, found himself back at the bedside of the king. This time, he thought he might as well ask his dumb questions. Dumb question number one: "What ails you?" Dumb question number two: "What purpose does it serve?" As soon as he got the second question out of his mouth, the wound healed right before his eyes. At the same instant, the wasteland was transformed. Grass turned green, crops started to grow, people came back to life, and baby animals began being born all over the place.

"So what does it mean?" asks the lady with the chain. "The Amfortas wound represents the illusion of separateness, the notion that a human being is nothing but a skin-encapsulated bag of meat and bones, dragging around a dreary little ego and separated by his or her hide from the rest of the natural world. People who buy into this belief tend to live what Thoreau called 'lives of quiet desperation.' The wasteland.

"Question number one let the king know he wasn't totally isolated. Someone cared enough to reach out and inquire about his health. Question number two was a revelation. Every single healer the king had consulted began by asking what caused the wound. In the mind of the king, the idea that his suffering might be serving some real purpose closed the imaginary gap between himself and the rest of the natural world. That healing transformed the king's life experience from a wasteland into a happy, productive place."

The psychologist now introduces a kahuna medicine woman who says that when people come to her looking for healing, she begins by asking Parsifal's two questions. "Everyone answers the first, no problem. If the second one stumps them, I send them out into nature to find an answer. I might tell them to sit under a tree or something like that. Like mana from heaven, the answer always comes and it's always a revelation."

Kahuna tradition sees the manifest world as an integrated, interconnected ecosystem. A single happening. I like that. I like it a lot better than seeing it as a mindless machine powered by a couple of cosmic mainsprings

11

called cause and effect. If what I see is what I get, I might as well look at the real world the way the kahunas do and see it as an expression of an intelligent, friendly energy that is rigged in my favor. It's a much prettier picture.

The next morning, refreshed and optimistic, I fly to the big island of Hawaii. Wonder after wonder continues to unfold.

2

One Plus One

If you ain't got a strong woman by your side, get one!
A CORPORATE EXECUTIVE

Makapala. The retreat ground. In the assembly hall, about fifty people are standing around, chatting and waiting for the session to start. A VW Rabbit pulls up in front of the building and a wiry little guy with big ears hops out and scurries in. It's Reverend Jerry. He keeps looking at his watch and muttering, "I'm late. I'm late. I'm really quite late." He grabs me by the arm, hauls me across the hall, and parks me in front of this woman who's standing by herself.

"This is Susan," he says without taking his eyes off his watch. "I think you two should meet. Don't ask me why. I have no idea. If you will excuse me, I really must run. I'm really quite late. The session should have started half an hour ago." He bounces off, leaving us standing there, looking at each other. We make some small talk, and when it's time for me to start the seminar, I give her a hug and we go our separate ways. I have no idea why I hugged her. I do know it felt good. It still does.

"We really must stop meeting like this."

There she is—brown-eyed Susan. Right behind me in the chow line, smiling. I smile back and turn to fill my coffee cup. When I turn around, she's gone. The next morning, as Reverend Jerry and I are finishing breakfast, I look up and there she stands again. I get the feeling she's flashing on and off like one of those neon signs. Now I see her, now I don't. This time, she doesn't even look at me. Just wants to know from Jerry where she can find a pair of Ping-Pong paddles. He tells her and off she goes again. Oh well, out of sight, out of mind. I think I'll walk on the beach.

Soft sand underfoot, sun sparkles dancing on crystal clear water, exotic birds singing in gently swaying palms. Tropical paradise. Who could be bummed out in a place like this? Looks like I could. I'm feeling isolated and alone. Cut off from everything and everyone I ever knew. The empty beach looks barren and desolate. The wasteland. I wonder what ails me. The sun is getting hot. Last thing I need now is a sunburn.

Sitting in the shade of a friendly palm tree, I try watching myself breathe, hoping it will improve my mood. Breathing out, I wonder what purpose does it serve, this sense of isolation. As I'm breathing in, the word *growth* pops into my mind. Is this tree talking to me telepathically? Let's pretend it is. Like people who make believe they know what their pets are thinking. It comes to me that for most people growth usually takes place outside the comfort zone. Breathing out, I wonder why. Breathing in, I flash on the word *resistance.* Where did that come from? Same place all thoughts come from. No place and everyplace. Mana from heaven. A revelation. It strikes me that growth is change. Generally, we humans tend to mistrust change. It rattles our cage. So we resist.

This requires effort. Resistance and effort push us outside the comfort zone. Not growth.

A coconut falls from the tree and lands at my feet. This reminds me of a quote by a poet Reverend Jerry was talking about this morning. "Despise that which must be achieved through effort and watch for what falls into your lap through a miracle." The coconut could have hit me on the head. But it didn't. Looking at what's happening in terms of purpose, rather than cause, leads me to believe my tree friend didn't mean to hurt me—just to jog my memory. After all, it is alive and, according to kahuna tradition, conscious.

I realize that if I choose to grow now and enjoy the changes, I can bypass effort and resistance and notice the miracles. Suddenly the beach looks beautiful and full of life. The wasteland is transformed.

Lunchtime. Except for some volunteers behind the food counter, the cafeteria is empty.

"I like being old. I like living alone." This from a bubbly little lady as she scoops soup into a bowl and sets it on my tray. Her name tag says "Thelma." I'm not sure who she's talking to.

"Nowadays I get to do whatever I feel like doing," she starts up again. "Whenever I feel like doing it. I used to make myself miserable fussing about how happy I would be if only things were different. Then I heard this corny song about going to sleep counting blessings instead of sheep. Well, I tried it and let me tell you, it changed my life.

"When I see what's right with the world instead of

what's wrong with it, it looks a lot brighter. Accentuate the positive, eliminate the negative. That's what I always say. What do you always say?" She's talking to me. Without waiting for an answer, she sets the dessert beside my soup, gives me a wink, and says, "Sit wherever you like, honey. Pick a place, expect a miracle, and watch what happens."

What an odd thing to say. But then, since my divorce, everything seems odd. That's just what's so. So I might as well do as Thelma says. Relax, enjoy, and go with the flow. As for blessings, I'm in good shape. What with a free trip to Hawaii, a new house, a new car, and all. If only I had someone to share it with. I can sit wherever I like. I don't have to go back to the minister's table. Jerry won't mind. He'd be pleased to see me mingle. After all, that's what you're supposed to do when you're single.

Something tells me I should pay attention to what's happening here. That I'm about to make one of those seemingly insignificant choices that turn out to have a profound effect on the direction of a person's life. What is that something and how does it know? Jerry calls it divine guidance. He says it is a communication from Spirit, which is the source of everything so it knows everything. Sounds a lot like the kahuna idea of mana from heaven.

About a hundred places to pick from. My eyes scan the scene until on the inside something says, "That one." I plunk my tray onto the table, myself into the chair, and wait.

And here she is again—sitting at the same table. Her friends are gaping at me with openmouthed amazement. It seems I picked the place directly opposite the one where she's been taking her meals since the start of the retreat. Her friends are surprised because she told them she had a hunch something like this might happen. One thing leads to another, and when we're all packed and ready to leave, I hear myself asking if maybe I could come home with her so we could spend a little more time together.

It feels as if there are two people in here. One asking, the other hearing. Have you ever noticed that one part of you does things while another part watches?

Anyway, she says okay, and I get to meet a few more of her friends: Angel, a pedigreed pit bull with gentle eyes, a constant smile, and a heart of gold. Pinky, a Flame Point Himalayan cat with a whole collection of blue ribbons from cat shows. And a shaggy dog named Wally Brown with a personality that's part dolphin, part monkey. All went well during our brief visit together. Then off I went to my new home and my new life in Honolulu.

About ten days later, Simonton Worthington T-Bird and I pop down to the Honolulu airport to pick up Susan, who's flown over for a visit. When she appears at the baggage claim area, I'm surprised at how pleased I am to see her. There's that split again. Someone in here seems to like her. That surprises another someone, the one who's really leery about long-term relationships and emotional entanglements. The one who, as it turns out, is in for an even bigger surprise.

17

Back at the house, she has no sooner settled in than Susan makes an announcement. "There's something I think you ought to know. Recently, I decided it's time for me to be married. I drew up a list of characteristics of the man I'd like to live with. Lucky for you, you fit the description. I'm talking about a committed, monogamous relationship. To me, that's what marriage means. If it isn't you, it'll be someone like you. I've decided that there are ten thousand guys out there who are exactly right for me. I intend to let them into my life one at a time until I find a relationship that works great.

"I do like you a lot and enjoy being with you. So even if you're not interested in the possibility of marriage, we can still spend a few wonderful days together and I think we'll always be good friends. I feel such a closeness with you already." She stops for a minute to let the words sink in. "I can't believe I'm telling you all this. It's coming right through me. Totally out of my control, but there it is." Another pause and then, "There's no hurry. Take your time. Whichever way you decide is fine with me. I'm willing to wait the whole five days of my visit with you for an answer."

The logical analyzer in me is flabbergasted. A live-in companion is one thing. But a wife, that's a horse of another color. Inside me, he's ticking off a hundred reasons why this is not a good idea. I can always count on him to come up with a hundred reasons why anything out of the ordinary is not a good idea. Change upsets him. The little kid in me loves Susan's animal friends, knows she's fun to be with, and is more than willing to do whatever it takes to keep her around. The incurable romantic in me thrives on relationship and enjoys being married. But the logical analyzer has his heels dug in. "No way," says he. "Just get me out of this."

Something tells me I should go get the mail. Might as well—my mind is blown anyway. There is just one item in the mailbox, and it's addressed to me. A communication from a Sufi poet who has been dead for who knows how long. This three-line poem by Rumi is on the front of a flyer announcing a seminar on enlightenment in L.A. It begins:

Forgetting closes the door.
The sound of the door opening
awakens the sleeping woman.

The flyer's bottom line leaps off the page and hits me in the eye:

Fantastic! Do not let a chance like this go by.

We don't. Before the lease on Lucille's place runs out, Susan and I are woman and husband. Today, we're pleased to say, we're alive and well, living happily ever after in the Pacific Northwest.

The story of how we made each other up pushes the limit of what you may have been led to believe is possible in the real world. Pushing limits stretches the mind. Stretching the mind, like stretching the body, feels good and keeps you limber.

3

The Reality Fantasy

As soon as you think you know how things really are,
find another way of looking at them.
ROBIN WILLIAMS

Let's begin with a delicious little stretch of the mind—
artificial reality machines. You might even consider
them to be giant adult toys for the kid in you.

Virtual reality, as he calls it, is the brainchild of a
thirty-year-old computer wiz from Silicon Valley, California. Reality, as he sees it, is the world we experience
through our eyes, ears, skin, and other sense organs. If
you cover these organs with computerized clothing and
cut them off from stimuli originating in what he calls
"the outside world," that reality disappears. We must
point out that this happens to us every night without
help from any kind of clothing. Our sense organs shut
themselves down and the outside world disappears. After a while, they turn themselves on again and transmit
a new set of stimuli. As a result, we find ourselves in
another world—the dream world. Computerized clothing does the same thing. It subjects your sense organs to
an alternate set of stimuli, except these are programmable. You can program a dream for yourself and dream
it while you're wide awake. The images you see are three-
dimensional and in living color. The sounds you hear
are stereophonic and digitally programmed. You can't

tell either from the real thing. What's more, you can move around in this world just the way you can in actual time and space.

A reporter from National Public Radio described his experience inside one of these gadgets, which consist of computerized goggles, headphones, and gloves with motion-sensing computer chips: "I put them on and here I am, in a kitchen with a ticking clock on the wall. Everything looks and sounds absolutely real. Except that there's a hand drifting around in here. I can tell it's my hand because when I wiggle my fingers, it wiggles right along with me. But it, the virtual hand, seems to have supernatural powers. If I point my finger at the clock, I find myself flying toward it. As it turns out, there are no laws of physics in here to keep me from flying right into it. There is nothing inside but an empty white space. So I turn around and find myself looking down at the kitchen from inside the clock. There is a second hand ticking around right in front of my nose. Only I don't seem to have a nose.

"There's no doubt about it. This is strange. I ask the inventor what purpose can all this serve, and he punches a few keys on the computer.

"The stove top loses touch with gravity and floats up to hover under the ceiling fan. So I fly over to it, grab it with my virtual hand, and set it down beside the sink where it belongs.

"The inventor tells me the space agency is creating virtual worlds representing outer space right here on Earth. The idea is that an operator flies up to a virtual satellite, fixes it with his virtual arm, and his movements are relayed to a robot arm that actually is in outer space. So we can work on a satellite or a space station on Mars without ever leaving home."

So much for practical applications. Beyond that, there are mind-boggling implications. According to its creator, the invention of virtual reality requires that we stretch an understanding of what reality is.

"Virtual reality machines," says the inventor, "create an experience you can call a dream, an alternate reality or a different world. The only limit is the imagination of the programmer. The question arises, are these real images? To answer that question, you must make up your mind about what you believe reality actually is. But as I see it, the only difference between dreams and reality is just that we can share reality with other people. With computerized clothing, two people or twenty or two thousand can enter and be in the same world together. It's just a computer program that anyone with the proper equipment can plug into. What's more, you can give people the power to create their world, to build it and change it while they are in it. It's just a matter of computer programming. The world they jointly create and share is not going to be a simulation, not a dream, not an illusion. It is, in fact, reality."

The main thrust of this argument is that the worlds created and experienced in virtual reality machines are as real as the one we ordinarily live in because they are shared sensory experiences. Plus they're programmable. We're looking at the possibility that consensus reality, the place we call the real world, is also programmable. This possibility seems more real if you think of the brain in your head as a single unit in a global network of interconnected reality generators. You can use yours to create, plug into, or share any reality you like. The National Public Radio program continued with a university professor's view of reality. She told a Hindu folktale that went something like this: A farmer and a guru are walking beside a lake. The farmer asks the guru how he can know for sure what's real. The guru says reality cannot be described. Only experienced. The farmer asks how, and the guru tells him to go jump in the lake, so he does. Next thing the farmer knows, he's lying in the grass with his aching head cradled in a young man's lap. The young man is weeping bitter tears, rocking back and forth, calling him Lyla, kissing him on the face and mouth, and pleading with him to please wake up. As he slowly regains consciousness, the farmer becomes aware that he's wearing a dress. That he has, in fact, turned into a woman.

In the course of conversation, Lyla learns that this young man is her fiancé. He says they were running through the woods when she tripped and banged her head on a rock. He rushes her into an emergency room, where she tells the doctor she has no recollection of her life up to this point except for some vague dream about being a farmer in another time and in another place. The doctors decide she's suffering from amnesia caused by a blow to the head. They tell her she may or may not get her memory back so she might as well go about the business of living her life starting right now.

Her fiancé drives her home and introduces her to a bunch of strangers who say they are her friends and relatives. After a year or so of settling in and getting used to the new order of things, Lyla marries her young man. A year after that, she gives birth to a daughter, who grows up, marries, and has a son of her own. When the child is three years old, their country gets involved in a war, in the course of which everyone in the family except Lyla and the grandson are killed. After a series of harrowing experiences, the two find safe haven in a neutral country, where Lyla raises Seb and puts him through medical school. Many years later, at the age of 102, Lyla suffers a stroke and summons her grandson to her bedside so she can bid him farewell. With Seb holding her hand, she closes her eyes and breathes her last.

Then, she opens them again to find herself lying on the grass with a throbbing headache and a lump on her left temple. Seb is still holding her hand, but he doesn't seem to know who she is. That's because she's a man again, that same farmer who was walking with the guru. Seb tells him that when he jumped into the lake, he bumped his head on a rock and knocked himself out. "Lucky I happened to be walking by. Your friend and I pulled you out. You'll have a headache for a day or so, but aside from that, I think you'll be just fine."

The farmer tells Seb he looks familiar and asks him if he had a grandma named Lyla. "I sure did," says Seb. "She raised me after my parents were killed in the war. Did you know her?" The farmer nods, and the guru smiles.

Both Seb and the farmer had personal experience of Lyla. Does that make her real? Suppose Seb had been killed in the war. Would she still be real?

To answer that question, you have to decide what, in your opinion, makes something real. Many people say, "If I can touch it, it's real." Applying that standard, we have to say that the clock and the stove top the reporter was describing were illusions because they didn't stimulate his sense of touch. Artificial reality machines can't do that yet. If you turned on the tap, the water running into the sink would look and sound real, but it wouldn't feel wet. You might see and hear eggs frying on the stove, but you wouldn't be able to smell or taste them, so you might say the kitchen isn't real no matter how many people see it simultaneously.

What about rainbows? Almost everyone has seen a real one or a picture of one. But you can't touch, taste, hear, or smell them. They only stimulate one of our senses. Does that mean they're illusions? What about light itself? Is that real?

We'd like to consider the possibility that reality is determined by personal choice. People, to some extent, select what they choose to believe is real. If this is the case, it seems quite logical to choose a reality structure that makes life better.

One day, Sara had to be in San Francisco. This meant driving across the Golden Gate Bridge, something she swore she would never do. The thought of losing control and going over the edge scared her half to death. Unreasonable as it was, the fear was as real as the bridge.

Changing either the fear or the bridge was out of the question. What could be changed was her perception. When she was little, Sara made believe pumping the pedals on her tricycle made the ground fly back under the rolling wheel. It struck her that she could make believe pressing the car's accelerator would do the same for the roadway on the bridge. As silly as it seemed, she decided to try it. Of course, she was kidding herself. Using a childish fantasy to solve a grown-up problem in the real world. The fact is, it worked. Keeping that image in mind allowed her to drive across and back without fear or panic.

Another fact, according to Albert Einstein, is that absolute motion is impossible to determine. That is to say, there is no way of knowing which is really moving. The car, the bridge, or both. It has to do with relativity theory.

When we were kids, we could look up at the sky and see things moving around up there. The sun, stars, moon, clouds. Then, we got sent to school and were told not to believe our eyes. We were instructed to believe that the spectacle of the sun and stars rising, traveling across the sky, and setting is an illusion, that they are really sitting still while we are watching them from the surface of this humongous ball of earth spinning in space. However, the clouds and the moon, they told us, look as though they're moving because they really are. If Einstein is right, nobody can possibly know what's really going on out there.

Henry Wadsworth Longfellow said, "Things are seldom

what they seem." What things are is called *reality*. How they seem is called *perception*. Your beliefs determine how the two relate to each other. A good example is when we think what we hear is what the other person really meant to say, like the store clerk when Brenda and Bert came in to buy a pet.

"I'd like to get a parakeet for my husband," Brenda told the clerk. Eyeing Bert, he responded. "Good thinking, Madam, but we don't make trades."

Another example is believing that what we see is what's really out there. Look at Figure 1 and guess which line is longer. Now, measure them. The ruler shows they are both the same length.

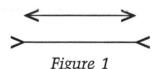

Figure 1

Which are you going to believe, some ruler or the evidence of your own eyes? Maybe they're both right.

John Broomfield, professor and historian, said that the distinctions made between observer and observed are not valid and that this understanding, coming as it does out of the natural sciences, demands that people re-examine the basic presuppositions of our civilization. A presupposition, a belief, is a set way of seeing the world. Different cultures have different beliefs, so they live in different worlds.

A colleague who was an army doctor in Vietnam told

us that in many villages, when a child dies they loosely tie a young animal to the grave site with a piece of string. They believe that in the night, the spirit of the child enters the animal's body. The creature then works itself loose and, with the child's spirit alive and well within it, runs off into the jungle to start a new life. The villagers don't try to prove that's what really happens. They just believe it. That belief has the power to comfort next of kin and ease their grief.

People from other cultures who chose to believe that being realistic and facing facts is more important than being comfortable and feeling at ease would call this belief a superstitious cop-out. An escape from reality. However, denying beliefs that create comfort and ease can lead to discomfort and disease. Besides, how can anyone prove that the child's spirit doesn't actually enter the body of the animal?

When something cannot be proved or disproved, we're free to believe whatever we choose. In cases like this, we might as well select the belief that makes us feel best.

Feelings seem to happen "in here," within the skin. That's because we were taught in school to believe that the skin is a boundary that separates two distinct worlds, one "in here" and one "out there." Flip Wilson, the comic, used to say, "What you see is what you get." That's a perfect summation of what scientists are saying today about the relationship between perception and reality. Namely, that how you choose to see the world creates the kind of world you get to live in. You can choose to believe that "in here" is every bit as real as "out there."

When she was in third grade, Cindy could close her eyes and be in a magic castle. To her mind, the castle was as real as the classroom. The teacher said it wasn't. When she asked him why, he said, "Because I said so." This is a classic example of how beliefs get handed down from generation to generation through word of mouth. Now, with an advanced degree in physics and a professorship at a prestigious university, Cindy can explain logically what she always knew intuitively.

"The real world," she tells her students, "is like the pea in the old shell game. Now you see it, now you don't."

She puts a pea on her desk and covers it with half a walnut shell. Then she asks if anyone can tell her where the pea is right now. Some of the students say it's on the desk under the shell. She asks them to prove it and they pick up the shell. Sure enough, there's the pea just the way it was before. That proves it was there all the time. Right?

"Wrong," says the professor. "That was then. This is now. One has nothing to do with the other. There was a pea on the desk before I covered it. There is a pea on the desk now that you've uncovered it. But this says nothing about the time in-between.

"Look at it this way. When I open the door to my refrigerator, the light is on. If I close it for a while and open it again, the light is on just the way it was before. Does that prove it was on all the time? Of course not. When I close the door, I presume, if everything is working right, that the light goes out. But where? Out of existence? It just vanishes into thin air? Pure magic?

"Applying the principles of quantum theory, I could presume that closing the door makes the food, the shelves, and everything else in there go out along with the light. After all, how can you prove they don't? Besides, presuming that they do makes my world work better. It might make yours work better, too."

Let's take a moment here to look at quantum theory—leaps through space and time. A quantum leap in space is what happens when something goes from here to there without ever existing anywhere in-between. The pea in the old shell game and the stuff in the refrigerator make quantum leaps through time. They go from then to now. If you'd like to see a quantum leap with your own eyes, try this:

1. Make a fist and point your index finger at the sky.
2. Place the base of the extended finger on the tip of your nose and close one eye.
3. Focus your open eye on the opposite wall or some object in the room. Notice where the finger is in relation to it.
4. Switch eyes and watch your finger make a quantum leap. Notice as you switch that one finger disappears as the other appears.

That's how it is with our inner and outer worlds. Switching one on turns the other off. Like an AM/FM radio.

Cindy knew that back in third grade. The white rabbit who lived in her magic castle told her. He said the castle was just as real as the classroom. To prove his point, the rabbit taught Cindy how to blur her eyes and make "out there" disappear, teacher and all. Teacher decided Cindy was nearsighted and told her mom to get her fitted with corrective lenses. The rabbit told Cindy the lenses were pieces of the mirror Alice went through to get into Wonderland.

"There's a magic world inside those little glass circles," he said. "Just set them on your nose and in you go, eyes first. You must be very careful not to get trapped in there. This can happen if you decide that what you're looking at with your eyes open is more real than what you see when your eyes are closed."

Professor Cindy, Professor Broomfield, and a growing number of scientists agree with the rabbit. They are telling us that the "real" (out there) world is exactly like the "imaginary" (in here) world. Put it out of your mind and, poof, it's gone. Writing in *Scientific American* magazine, Professor Bernard D'Espagnat of the University of Paris said, "The widely held belief that the real world consists of separate objects whose existence is independent of human consciousness is incompatible with quantum theory and conflicts with facts established by experiment."

Does that surprise you? Well, now you know how people must have felt when the widely held belief that the world is flat was first questioned. We are not saying the world "out there" isn't real. It's as real as it ever was, but no more real than the world "in here." So an imaginary castle is every bit as real as a brick schoolhouse. Here's why.

The basic building block of the schoolhouse is a brick. Break that down as far as you can, and you wind up with a grain of sand, the smallest part of which is an atom. Until recently, atoms were supposed to be the basic building blocks of everything. They were also supposed to have a life of their own, bouncing around in time and space like a bunch of billiard balls, doing their own thing whether or not anyone was aware of them. Theoretically, that made them and everything constructed of them real. Then, scientists smashed the atom and unwittingly shattered the illusory separateness of observer and observed.

In the debris, all they could find were the trails of subatomic particles swimming around in a sea of atomic energy. These particles, they say, are so small they can only be imagined. To us, that means they exist only in the mind of the observer. What's more, they have a habit of going on and off like lights. Observation turns them on. When no one pays them any mind, they go off. So, we could say that a brick schoolhouse, like every other thing, is an accumulation of imaginary particles generated by the human mind . . . which is what imaginary castles are made of.

The notion that the real world and the dream world are made of the same stuff is not new. "The Diamond Sutra," a five thousand–year-old religious text, describes the real world in terms remarkably similar to those of Dr. D'Espagnat.

Thus shall you think of this fleeting world—
A star at dawn, a bubble in a stream,

A flash of lightning in a summer cloud,
A phantom, an illusion, a dream.

Compare this to the traditional children's song that tells kids:

Row, row, row your boat, gently down the stream.
Merrily, merrily, merrily, merrily.
Life is but a dream.

Albert Einstein said it's okay to assume life is just a dream because, logically, there is no way to prove it isn't. The Taoist philosopher Lao-tzu looked at life exactly the same way. One night, he dreamed he was a butterfly. From then on, he said he couldn't shake the feeling that who he was was a butterfly dreaming it was a Taoist philosopher.

Any concept on which an ancient Chinese sage and a modern American physicist can see eye to eye over a span of fifty centuries deserves to be taken seriously. The notion that the real world isn't objectively real has been around for a long time, and it's making a big comeback today. Just considering the possibility that it's all a dream could change your life for the better.

Next time you're in a tough situation, try running that children's ditty through your head, the one about rowing your boat gently down the stream. Keep in mind that it may all be happening on the backs of your eyeballs. You might be surprised at how much better this can make you feel in a stressful situation.

Spiritual teachers tell us to look beyond appearances

to see the truth. The truth, according to them, and according to a growing number of experts at the cutting edge of scientific research, is that OBSERVER AND OBSERVED ARE ONE. In an unexpected meeting of the minds, both are telling us that reality may be in the eye of the beholder—a matter of perception. Perceptions are signals that our five senses send to our brains. There, they arrange themselves into patterns we interpret as reality. Then, with our minds, we project that reality "out there."

Now, what triggers the sense organs in the first place? Plato's Parable of the Cave deals with this question. It's about a tribe of cave dwellers who never go outside. Sitting in the cave with their backs to the opening on a bright sunny day, they watch the play of shadows on the walls and floor of the cave and argue about what's really out there causing them. The cave represents the inside of the human skull. The cave dwellers are "the observer" watching a play of perceptions (nerve impulses in the circuitry of the brain), trying to figure out what "the observed" is. Under the circumstances, all they can do is guess. If a guess is repeated often, it becomes a belief. Then, a fascinating thing happens. BELIEF INFLUENCES PERCEPTION.

Consider what happens if you change the color on two cards in an ordinary deck by printing the five of hearts in black and the six of clubs in red. Research has shown that people will never notice it. Even after you tell them what you did, most people will still see the traditional color scheme. People tend to see what they expect to see. Such is the power of belief.

Many people have a strong belief in a personal god. For those people, that god becomes a living reality. On the individual level, at least, BELIEF CREATES REALITY.

This explains what educators call "the Pygmalion effect." *Pygmalion* is a story about an English professor who converts a cockney guttersnipe into an active member of British high society. In a landmark experiment, psychologists matched the professor's accomplishment by turning dumb kids into smart ones. They selected a group of children with low achievement test scores and altered the results to make them look smart. The doctored records caused their new teachers to think they were dealing with exceptionally bright students. Sometime later, they were retested and got high scores just the way their teachers expected they would.

When we say belief creates reality, does that mean the Earth was really flat when everyone thought it was? Not necessarily. Only for those who believed it was. If you believe something is beautiful, impossible, or inevitable, then for you, it is. CHANGE YOUR BELIEF AND YOUR REALITY CHANGES.

When Phillip came in for his first counseling session, he was bent over, leaning heavily on a cane and hanging on to his wife's arm so he wouldn't fall down. We asked him how long he had been like that. He said it started about six months ago, when he turned eighty-five. "I guess when you get to be my age," he said, "you have to expect that your body won't work so well."

"You're not eighty-five," said his wife. "You're seventy-five." Phillip demanded to know how come she was so sure. "Your birth certificate. We sent for it when we applied for Social Security. Remember? According to that, you're only seventy-five years old. When we get home, I'll show it to you, and you can see for yourself."

What happened next was like one of those miracle cures you sometimes see on Sunday TV. Without a word, Phillip stood up straight, handed his wife the cane, and strode out of the room like a man who just had ten years subtracted from his age. He didn't have to shed ten years to do that. He could have simply shed the belief that with advancing age, the body falls apart.

If you're like most people we know, there are some things you check regularly to see if they need changing, like the clothes on your back or the oil in your car. It's probably a good idea to do the same with your beliefs, because, like anything else, they need changing from time to time. Since the only thing in this life we can count on is constant change, it's a safe bet to assume that what we think we now know is bound to turn into what we used to believe.

We used to believe the Earth was flat. Now, we choose to believe it's round. That's because people who are supposed to know about such things say it is. We call this a low-intensity belief because it has little effect on daily life. We also used to believe our world was the immovable center of the universe. Not so, say the experts. What we see with our eyes and feel in our bodies is wrong. We really live on a ball of earth that is spinning around at a thousand miles an hour as it zips around the sun at an even faster clip. Do you believe this? Why? How does believing it or not affect your day-to-day life experience?

Going from believing Mother Earth is flat and stationary to believing she's round and moves is called a paradigm shift. Actually, it's two. Now there's a third one. It says the real world isn't actually "out there" separate from you. It may be that you and everything "out there" are one entity, interconnected facets of a single system. This is a high-intensity belief. Opening your mind far enough to allow that it might be true could transform your life.

Someone once asked Albert Einstein what, in his opinion, was the most important question facing humanity today. His answer was, "Is the universe friendly?" Suppose, for the sake of argument, we accept the new paradigm and allow that reality is but a series of perceptions programmed by belief. Then, the answer to Einstein's question is obvious. If you believe the universe is friendly, then for you it is. If, on the other hand, you're a believer in Murphy's law and expect that anything that can possibly go wrong probably will, for you it probably will. You can believe whatever you like. We are suggesting that it might be a good idea to pay attention to what kind of life these beliefs create. The bottom line is this: IF BELIEF PROGRAMS REALITY, WHY NOT PROGRAM A LIGHT ROMANTIC COMEDY INSTEAD OF LIVING A HEAVY TRAGEDY?

4

The Real You

When you believe it, you'll see it.
WAYNE DYER

A beautiful child comes into the doctor's office. Sticking out of the center of her forehead is a huge green bullfrog.

"My God!" says the doctor. "How did such a horrible thing happen to a magnificent little creature like you?"

"I dunno, Doc," croaks the frog. "It started with a wart on my web."

This story is an allegory. The frog is the ego. The creature we think we need to get along in this world and survive. Along the same line, warts would be personality traits or physical characteristics we dislike in ourselves. They disfigure the frog. The beautiful child, the real self, is who we become when we accept ourselves just the way we are.

Allow yourself to believe what you are about to read. Try it on and see how it feels. If it feels like something you'd like to believe about yourself but can't quite manage to, consider the evidence we presented in the previous chapter—especially the experiments about how belief creates personal reality. Read it through twice a day for two weeks. See what happens in your personal experience. If you like the results, make reading it a permanent habit!

I am now and always have been perfect
I can do and be whatever I want to do or be
I love and have been loved and am loving
I recognize this and accept this
I can aspire to and have a higher state of awareness and
  consciousness
It is all right for me to do this

I live in a friendly universe which is unfolding as it
  should
I view the events and people in my life as opportunities for learning and know that I am the source of my
  experience
I know that at any moment I have the power to transform the quality of my life
I know that my attitude determines my experience

I am now and will continue to be increasingly alive,
  aware, and joyous
I know that my life is my responsibility and I create
  every moment and live in the moment
I, therefore, choose to live my life experiencing fully,
  in each moment, all that I create . . . infinite love,
  total health, unlimited joy, and perfect peace

I offer the world love and peace and accept love and
  peace in return
I take credit for the good I create within myself and all
  around me
I believe in myself and know that my clear intention
  is a magic wand
I can do and be whatever I want to do or be

The Real You

There's an old Cajun saying: "Be what you is." It has been a favorite of ours since we first heard it.

Actually, we're all brilliant. We're all surrounded by abundance. We all have things that go right for us every day. It's just that sometimes we forget to notice.

If we take time out each day from the busyness and the "to do" lists of our lives, we can get to know ourselves better. Begin by looking at personal successes, big and small. Even the "little wins" in a day, like a cleanup job well done or a new insight that our body's fine just the way it is, can be a good start.

We all have a wealth of talents and abilities. We often use them without even being aware of these great gifts. Our ability to balance, on many levels, is not just a talent. It's an ongoing miracle! Consider all the others.

Contemplating a day's "little wins" and ongoing miracles gives us a glimpse of the glory of what "we really is."

5

Playing the Game

Follow your bliss.
JOSEPH CAMPBELL

"What's going on out there, Jack?" Karl Pribram was on the phone with his son, the physicist.

"Hang on," said the voice on the other end. "I'll go see." A few seconds later, Jack came back and said, "It's raining."

Karl said he wasn't calling to inquire about the weather but about the nature of time-space reality. The stuff that stimulates our sense organs to create perceptions. What exactly is that? The answer to the question "What's that out there?" is something physicists have been looking for since their science first got started. Jack said as far as he can tell, all that's out there are waves. Not things, just waves.

Dr. Pribram, formerly of the department of neuropsychiatry at Stanford, had spent much of his life trying to answer the question "Who's this in here asking what's that out there?" Blending Jack's answer with his own expertise, he came up with a theory to explain how waves of energy become perceptions of people, places, and things. Stereophonic sound is a good model.

Out of the speakers and into your ears come vibrations, energy waves. There they get transformed and become electrical impulses sloshing around in your brain.

43

Like ripples from pebbles dropped into opposite ends of a pan of water, they collide, combine, and create a new wave form, called an interference pattern, which spreads throughout the entire system. Your conscious mind reads this pattern and according to Dr. Pribram "projects it as if it were out there," in the empty space in between the speakers. Ripples of light energy entering your eyes go through the same process. We could use a finger trick like the one that helped you see a quantum leap to illustrate. Hold a finger up, about a foot in front of the end of your nose, and look at it with one eye. You'll see an image. Switch eyes and you'll see a slightly different image in another location. Now, open the closed eye and allow the ripples of light energy pouring in from left and right to collide and combine in your brain. A third image appears in the empty space in between the other two, which have vanished. Which is the real finger?

Dr. Pribram's holographic theory of brain function suggests that the three-dimensional image you see with both eyes open is a holograph, a projection into empty space of an interference pattern that exists only in your brain. That suggestion leads us to consider the possibility that time-space reality, the real world, is a three-dimensional color hologram with quadriphonic sound, generated in the circuitry of the human brain and "projected as if it were out there." This brilliant and empowering theory has profound implications for the daily life of every person.

If you are at the movies and see the shadow of a fly on the screen, you would assume the fly itself is on the projector lens. We have talked about how beliefs act as lenses that shape perceptions, the basic building blocks of experience. Now, we are looking at the possibility that these perceptions are projected from the inside out. So, if life is less than you would like it to be, the culprit is bound to be a belief. The place to deal with it is "in here" in the projector, rather than "out there" on the screen. Replacing the old, worn-out lens with a new one makes for a much prettier picture.

A belief is an educated guess about what is really so. When trying to decide whether to accept or reject any particular one, we believe pragmatism is the best policy. The acid test, as we see it, isn't "Is this true?" but "Will this work?" Which test you choose to use is important because, as the next story shows, truth and practicality don't always go hand in hand.

Brenda and Bert bought a mule. When Bert tried to put it into the shed, it wouldn't fit because its ears were too long. Bert figured they would have to take it back because he didn't have the tools to raise the roof on the shed or the heart to cut the ears off the mule. Brenda said that the shed had a dirt floor so maybe he could dig down a foot or so and get the mule in that way.

"Now, ain't that just like a woman!" Bert said. "It ain't his feet that's too long, honey. It's his ears."

Some things we learned in school about how the world works missed the boat in two ways. It's impossible to prove they are true, and believing they are doesn't make life easier. Take the notion that brains create consciousness. Do you believe that? Not everyone does, you know. Lots of people believe it may be the other way around. The practicality of this point of view was underscored for us when we heard a person of the Buddhist persuasion comment on the death of a loved one. "I grieve over my loss," she said, "but I am comforted because it makes me reflect on the impermanence of all things and I am happy for him because I know he has taken on a higher form." In her situation, people who buy into the theory that the brain secretes consciousness the way the skin secretes sweat would feel this woman's grief and yet, because of their belief, deny themselves the comfort and joy she expressed.

This is really too bad because the argument that conscious awareness is nothing but an accidental by-product of electrical activity in the brain, and is snuffed out when that stops, is pretty flimsy. If the brain is damaged, the body it is in reflects the extent of the damage. This proves that every body needs an intact, functioning brain to stay alive and well. Not that brains generate bodies.

The notion that brains generate consciousness is based on an even shakier line of reasoning. This is like saying that turning off a TV set interrupts the show. TV sets do not create shows. Shows come through them.

Consider the possibility that consciousness is the eternal observer. Maybe, the way light was around before lamps were, consciousness was around before there were brains. Brains serve it by transforming energy waves into perceptions—holograms—which it observes. Dr. Eugene Wigner, who won a Nobel prize in physics, told us he believes "consciousness may be all there is." If that is

46

so, the energy waves Jack Pribram was talking about would have to be ripples of consciousness. So life experience would turn out to be a matter of consciousness observing itself. Observer and observed would be one and the same.

What we have been calling consciousness, one of our clients calls "I AM–NESS." Your I AM–NESS is a state of being you encounter just this side of sleep. Before thoughts, emotions, and other perceptions start. Or, after they stop. Scientists call it "alpha state awareness." This emptying of the mind while wide awake is the goal of meditation. There is hard evidence this has healing powers. Formal meditation isn't the only way to get there. We all experience flashes of empty I AM–NESS all day long. It often happens right after you answer the phone. In the moment in between your "Hello" and the other party's response, your mind is alert, silent, receptive. Picture yourself in that situation right now. You'll get a sense of it.

Empty I AM–NESS, the real you, is exactly the same for everyone and has no known cause. It just is. Since it invented time, we could also say it always was. The more we identify with it, the better life gets. It is entirely possible that life itself may be a game invented by consciousness, I AM–NESS, for its own amusement. A computer game where brains are hardware, mind is software, and perception is printout. Remember that the acid test for a new idea is not "Is this true?" but "Will allowing that it might be true make life work better?" This one might. You be the judge.

Imagine the brain in your head is an infinitely powerful, interactive, user-friendly, living computer. Bear in
mind that comparing brains to computers is like comparing eagles and airplanes. One is alive, the other a
machine. In terms of performance, this makes a huge
difference. Our biocomputer brain operates in three
modes: thinking, imaging, and feeling. Each is a two-
way street. Thoughts, images, and feelings are languages
the brain uses to print out perceptions that I AM–NESS
observes and interprets. I AM–NESS uses these same
languages to program the computer and modify the printout. One example would be the rosy scenario technique
for programming a happy outcome to a potentially stressful situation.

A client called to say she was in a snit because she
just got a threatening letter from a health club she quit
three months ago for reasons of health. The letter, which
was actually a poor quality photocopy addressed to
"Dear Member," informed her that her membership had
been canceled, her initiation fee was forfeited, and unless she paid the three months' dues that were now in
arrears within ten days, her account would be turned
over for collection. This, in spite of the fact that she
had called in advance to let them know she was drop-
ping her membership. Needless to say, this ruined what
started out to be a really nice day. Thoughts about a bad
credit rating, lawyer's fees, and the injustice of it all
swirled around in her head and made her feel awful.

We suggested she could reprogram the whole experience by thinking of a best-case scenario with no bad

48

guys. After taking a couple of deep breaths to calm herself down, she admitted that maybe it was possible that what she got was a form letter sent to her by mistake. In that case, all she had to do was call the manager, explain what happened, and offer to provide a doctor's note. "Doctors' notes fix everything," she said. In her mind, she ran through the entire conversation, picturing the manager apologizing for the error and telling her to ignore the letter, he would take care of it.

Then, she called, explained her problem, and got into a pleasant conversation about how she and the manager were both amateur actors. When this was over, he told her that in the interest of community relations, he would wave the clause in her membership contract under which she agreed to give the club three months advance notice in writing of any intention to cancel her membership. Imagine how the affair would have turned out had she stuck to her original scenario about bloodsucking parasites looking for ways to extract money from the pockets of hardworking people and had called the manager in that frame of mind.

What we are doing here is writing a best-case scenario about the human condition by suggesting that reality is programmable and that we have more control over our own life experiences than the old objective reality belief system would lead us to believe.

The way we play it, the object of the life game is feeling good. As good as possible, for as long as possible, as often as possible. We keep score on a scale of one to ten. Ten is ecstasy. Zero is feeling no pain or pleasure.

Minus ten would be feeling bad enough to need intensive care. Beliefs constitute the rules of the game. We make them up as we go along and change them whenever we feel like. Switching from the worst-case to best-case scenario in any given situation is a good example of this gambit. The game is played situation by situation or, at the very longest, one day at a time, which is how Mahatma Gandhi played it. He said, "Every night, I give up the world totally. In the morning, I take it back on my own terms."

To start a game, you choose a belief. Any belief. This programs your biocomputer brain to project the life experience that accurately reflects and completely confirms that belief. Then you check to see, on a scale of one to ten, how it feels to live like that. If the score is lower than you'd like it to be, discard the old belief, pick a new one, and see if that works any better.

A client was planning a final visit to a dying friend. The very thought of it made her feel terrible—a minus five. She felt so bad because she believed physical death extinguishes personal consciousness. Suppose she decided to believe it doesn't. Suppose she believed that her friend was passing on to a beautiful new place where she would be peaceful and happy. Would that make her feel better?

"Sure," she said, "but I gave up believing nice people die and go to heaven about the same time I quit believing in Santa Claus. I must admit, I find these reports about near-death experiences interesting. You know, where people are clinically dead for a while and come back to say they left their bodies, went into a long, dark tunnel with a bright light at the end. Some of them said they felt so gloriously wonderful they didn't want to come back but were told they had to. My husband, he's an engineer, says it is pure poppycock. According to him, life is just an accidental flash of consciousness in between two eternal darknesses. He says people who believe anything else are just kidding themselves."

We asked how come he is so sure that this is so. She said because most experts say it is. We reminded her that there was a time when most experts said the world was flat, and she said she didn't know what to believe. Finally, she decided, since there is no way to know for sure what happens after a person's body dies, she could believe whatever she liked.

When she got to the hospital, it was obvious that for her friend, the end was very near. She took her by the hand and whispered, "Bon voyage" into her ear. The friend opened her eyes, whispered, "Thank you," and passed away leaving just the trace of a smile on her face.

Another client told us how a sudden change of belief dramatically improved her mother's sense of well-being and kept her feeling fine all through a catastrophic illness. "Mother had a stroke that left her paralyzed, so we had to put her in a nursing home. She was, by nature, an active, independent person, so being bedridden was very hard on her. She spent all her time praying for release from the useless prison of a body. One day, I came to visit her, and she was happy as a clam. Still paralyzed, but talking like her old self. She invited me to sit at the kitchen table and have some tea and cookies while she prepared lunch. Then, she kept chatting happily just as if she were bustling around playing hostess in her own home. I guess she had had another stroke and lost touch with reality. When I tried to tell her she was bedridden in a nursing home because of a stroke, she looked at me as if I were crazy. To this day, she thinks she is home living a normal life. I guess, in a way, you could say she is. Whenever I visit, I humor her. She thinks she is humoring me. It's the weirdest thing, but we get along."

At first, you might be tempted to believe the mother was hallucinating. Suppose we told you the daughter had a history of mental instability due to LSD overdose. What would you believe then? This is like asking you to decide whether the chicken or the egg came first. Since there is insufficient data to make a rational decision, you can believe whatever you like.

The chicken and egg question raises an interesting issue. The issue of black and white. The widespread belief that if one theory is right, its opposite has to be wrong. Creationists believe God created chickens and caused them to lay eggs in order to perpetuate the species. Believers in evolution claim that the egg came first. That the chicken is a device it uses to reproduce and evolve. A long time ago, they say, some reptile laid an egg that hatched out a birdlike creature that eventually evolved into a chicken. It is not a difference of opinion that brings the two sides into conflict. In fact, it is a shared belief—the notion that there is such a thing as absolute truth. Give it up, and there is nothing to argue about because then everybody can be right.

An effective technique for selecting beliefs that create a better life is scientific method. It works exactly like the life game we described earlier. Let's run an experiment to demonstrate the biocomputer brain theory using the method so you can see how it works.

The first requirement of scientific method is an open mind. Allow that the idea to be tested might be valid. Then, run a trial and see for yourself. We'll describe an experiment to test the idea that your biocomputer brain can create a favorable reality—that a clear mental image can program it to project the life experience that matches the image. You are welcome to try it and see if it works for you. Let's start with something simple. Like parking spaces.

When you get into your car, in your mind's eye see yourself getting out of it having parked where you want to. As you approach your destination, picture the empty parking spacc and imagine how good you will feel if this actually works. Really feel the satisfaction and sense of accomplishment. If you are in a congested area, picture a vehicle pulling out of a space you'd like to get into. Watch for it. Expect it to happen. Chances are, it will. It is important to keep an open mind and allow that it might, because negative thoughts instruct the computer to inhibit the process.

Once, we were driving down a busy street in central San Francisco, discussing this stuff with a skeptical friend. We were on a main traffic artery, so parking was severely restricted. "Tell you what," he said. "The Mark Hopkins Hotel is just ahead. If you can create a legal parking space anywhere on this next block, I'll buy you dinner." We pulled over to the empty curb within ten feet of the hotel entrance. Right under a sign that read, "No parking 8 A.M. to 4 P.M." The time was 3:58 P.M. Dinner was expensive and delicious.

Once you have got parking spaces down, you can go on to bigger and better things. Remember, making things happen and getting what you want is not the object of the life game. Feeling good is. Some people link the two by putting the cart before the horse. They tell themselves, "If only I had money, a relationship, a new car, or whatever, then I would feel good." So they buy books and take seminars on visual imagery, positive thinking, and goal setting. Sometimes they pray, repeat affirmations, or work as hard as they can to get what they think they need to make them feel good. It often works but seldom lasts. There are people who get everything they ever wanted and wind up feeling as bad as, if not worse than, they did before. This condition is far from rare and even has a name: destination sickness.

To get a feel for what destination sickness is like, consider the fact that every time you eat, you lose your appetite. When you are feeling hungry, you know, from past experience, that eating makes you feel good. So you do and it does, but not for long. Within hours, the emptiness, along with the urge to fill it, is back. Satisfying the urge to eat feels so good that some people decide there is no need to empty out and get hungry before

54

enjoying the pleasure. They keep on eating even after they have had enough. Then, what started out as a source of pleasure turns into a cause of pain. The pain is a signal to let them know that continuing to do what used to feel good a little while ago, even though it doesn't now, is counterproductive. Also, that emptying out is every bit as important as filling up. Recognizing that this applies to every aspect of life and agreeing to go along with it, we can avoid unnecessary pain and make the filling up times richer and more productive. If the phone isn't ringing when you think it is supposed to, if life insists on slowing down when you want it to keep going full steam ahead, consider the possibility that you are being guided to sit back and listen. Maybe the forces in our lives are gifts to be cherished.

To make the most of them, we must (1) notice them, (2) be thankful for them, and (3) use them wisely. Next time there is a lull in your life, try celebrating it. Thank the silent phone, the empty mailbox, or the absent partner for giving you the time to rest, rejuvenate, and catch up on the important things in life. Things like stargazing, thought watching, or that wonderful old hobby, horizontal meditation. This is when the magic happens.

Astronaut Ed Mitchell said an answer to the riddle of the universe came to him while idly staring out a window without a thought in his head. It happened soon after Apollo 14 cleared the orbit of the moon on its way back to Earth. All systems were on automatic, so there was nothing special he had to do. He just sat there, absentmindedly gazing out the spacecraft window. The ship was in a barbecue mode, rotating slowly so that the sun's rays would be evenly distributed over its surface. As he gazed out the window, the moon drifted by. Then the sun, then the Earth, and then the moon again. In the background was an unearthly profusion of stars set against the blackest black he had ever seen. Dr. Mitchell described what happened next as an explosion of awareness.

"I suddenly realized that it's all one. That this magnificent universe is a harmonious, directed, purposeful whole and that we humans both as individuals and as a species are an intimate part of the ongoing process of creation."

Dr. Mitchell's flash of insight summarizes beautifully the basic premise of this book. Like Albert Einstein, who was kicked out of high school in Germany for daydreaming and who said he didn't get to understand how the universe works by using his rational mind, Dr. Mitchell didn't figure this out. The revelation popped out of empty awareness while his rational mind was idling in neutral.

You don't have to fly to the moon to get an explosion of insight out of an empty mind. Newton and Buddha both got theirs under a tree. Like a bolt out of the blue, the concept of gravity struck Sir Isaac as he idly watched an apple fall. Sitting under a Bodhi Tree, doing absolutely nothing, Buddha got enlightened and saw that attachment is the source of all human suffering.

The philosopher Archimedes got it in the bathtub in ancient Greece. What he got was the answer to why some things float and some sink. Being a lover of knowledge, he was interested in things like that. The flotation puzzle had him stumped. One day, he decided to put the matter out of his mind, relax, and take a bath. As he settled into the tub, he noticed the usual rise in water level. Then it hit him—a quantum leap in consciousness. In a flash, he went from being stumped to knowing the answer. When you settle into a bath, your body pushes water out of your way. The displaced liquid moves to the top of the tub. That is the key. If an object on the surface displaces an amount of water that weighs at least as much as it does, it floats. If not, it sinks. Archimedes didn't figure this out; it was as if a light bulb lit up in his mind to illuminate something that was there all the time. It has been said that the old philosopher got so excited he ran stark naked and dripping wet through the streets of Athens yelling, "Eureka," a word that has come to be associated with the experience Zen Buddhists call satori. A flash of illumination that explodes out of empty I AM–NESS.

Science-fiction writer Ray Bradbury told an interviewer that his best story ideas come to him via this route. He said that if he is looking for new ideas and nothing is happening, he puts the whole thing out of his mind and occupies himself with other things. Then, he sleeps on it. First thing in the morning, he looks for the new ideas. They are always there, waiting for him.

Next time you find yourself wrestling with a tough problem that has got you tied up in knots, do what the geniuses do. Use your biocomputer brain as a tuner.

Relax and allow solutions to flow into it rather than trying to drag them out. What you need to tune into is
empty I AM–NESS, pure consciousness. To do this, you
need to turn off your thinker, which produces static and
inhibits the inflow of new information. Going to sleep
is the easiest way we know of to turn it off. You might
like to try Ray Bradbury's approach to deal with a problem you're trying to find the solution to right now. Sleep
on it. After you have settled into bed for the night, program your biocomputer brain to scan for the answer.
In the morning, when you first wake up, before thoughts,
emotions, and other perceptions start, look for it. Chances
are, it will be there.

We believe that programmed into each and every human brain, yours included, is the life experience of every creature that ever lived on earth. If one accepts the
basic tenet of morphogenetic field theory, which we
do, that is a perfectly reasonable thing to believe. The
theory is the brainchild of Rupert Sheldrake, a former
biology professor at Cambridge University in England.
As we understand it, he is suggesting that energy fields
exist before and aid in the creation of all physical entities. Like footprints on the sands of time or the smile
on the face of the Cheshire cat, they persist, as form-
generating fields, after the physical entity is gone. We
would like to point out in passing that Professor Sheldrake's hypothesis plugs a gaping hole in the genetic in-
heritance theory.

Throughout the ages, no one knew how fertilized eggs
and other seeds managed to produce life forms shaped

like their parents and predecessors. Then, a monk named Mendel figured out that it is all done with genes. Nowadays, conventional wisdom states that genes are to living things as blueprints are to finished products. This is confirmed by the fact that scientists can produce life forms with variant shapes by engineering genes to alter the blueprint. We just heard about a company in Australia that is trying to engineer a strain of blue roses using this method.

The map is not the territory. Likewise, the shape imprinted in the genes is not the three-dimensional life form. Professor Sheldrake's theory offers an explanation for how blueprints get converted into finished products. Consider the possibility that genes may generate energy fields that serve as invisible molds for living cells to grow into and be shaped by.

When we discussed parking spaces, we were talking about beliefs doing the same for life experiences by programming brains to generate energy fields that serve as invisible molds for physical forms to flow into. Think of the energy fields as ripples in an infinite ocean of awareness (I AM–NESS), which a character in *Star Wars* described as "that which surrounds us, penetrates us, and binds the galaxies together."

Following Professor Sheldrake's line of reasoning, we could say life experiences are imprinted as precursors and memories not only in individual brains but in the field of consciousness itself. Then, as brand new brains grow into the field (which may be all there is), they acquire these imprints along with physical form. Carl Jung

59

calls this field of knowledge "the collective unconscious," that is, the bottomless well of stuff we all know but don't know we know.

Here is a nice variation on Ray Bradbury's technique that uses the biocomputer's feeling mode to tap into the well and come up with right action in stressful situations. It involves pursuit of pleasure. If you are in a bind and can't find a way out, try putting the whole thing out of your mind and doing something just for fun. The feeling of pleasure created by this type of activity will lead to an unexpected resolution of the problem. A slightly doctored version of a Zen parable and two true stories from the files of the Transformation Learning Center show how well this works.

A Zen master was being chased by a bear when he went over the edge of a twenty-foot ledge. About halfway down, he landed on a tree branch, which broke his fall. The bear leaned over and tried to grab him. Her swipes barely missed the top of his head. He could easily have dropped the extra ten feet to the ground if not for the hungry tiger trying to grab him from below. Her claws just grazed the bottoms of his sandals. Then he saw a rattlesnake crawling toward him along the branch. Below the branch, well within his reach, was a clump of wild strawberries. Calmly, the master reached down, picked a plump red one, popped it into his mouth, and said aloud, "Mmmm, delicious!"

For some reason, this infuriated the bear, who lunged at him, lost her balance, and fell on the tiger. That started a battle royal, which scared off the snake and allowed the master to pick a few more strawberries, drop lightly to the ground, and go on his way.

The same strategy works well for ordinary people in difficult situations. If you ever feel caught between a rock and a hard place, with all of your options neutralized, instead of kicking, screaming, or spinning your wheels worrying, try giving up and doing something just for the fun of it. The results may surprise you. One of our clients was told he had to vacate his apartment by the end of the month because the building was about to be torn down. After weeks of hunting, every place he found was too small, too expensive, or both. D day was approaching, and he had no idea what to do next. Reluctantly, he agreed to put the problem out of his mind for twenty-four hours and spend the day doing something he loved to do. Biking in the country. On a back road, he ran across a sign that read "FOR SALE BY OWNER." By the end of the month, he was settling into a little cabin by a brook that suited his needs and his pocketbook perfectly.

After that, we worked with a young woman who had lost her job and wasn't able to find another. Her unemployment benefits were running out, and she was worried about winding up homeless. She had tried everything and by now was at the end of her rope, exhausted, and starting to panic. After we talked a while, she agreed that losing herself in a painting might make her feel better even if it didn't improve her situation. Scary as it was, she decided to splurge on a canvas and some paintbrushes even though, logically, she couldn't afford them.

At the art supply shop, she got into a conversation with the owner and an hour later had a well-paying job as manager.

How do you decide what to do at any given moment? Mostly, our behavior patterns are shaped by one of three options: (1) what we think we should do, (2) what we feel like doing, and (3) what is fun. Priority-wise, these options are usually arranged in that order. The people in the story we just told reversed the order and their lives changed. We believe reexamining options and re-ordering priorities can make almost anyone's life work better. To do this, you don't have to spend all of your waking hours having fun. Just realize that a minimum daily dose may be essential to your well-being—that PLEASURE IS A BIOLOGIC NECESSITY.

The American Declaration of Independence says that each of us has a God-given right to life, liberty, and the pursuit of happiness. Liberty is the right to do whatever we feel like doing whenever we feel like doing it. What kind of world do you think this would be if everyone lived like that? What kind of life do you think yours would be if you lived like that? Before answering, con-sider the fact that all life forms on our planet, except for us humans, do live like that. They have been around for millions of years longer than we have, so maybe they know something we don't.

It has been said, "Fish gotta swim, birds gotta fly." Probably for the same reason, human toddlers need to stand up and walk. They feel the urge and, as you know, satisfying an urge is like scratching an itch. Indescribably delicious. So we have decided to believe fish swim because it makes them feel good, and birds fly because it is fun. Also that feeling good and having fun are things we have to do in order to survive. Judging by their behavior, plants, animals, and children apparently know, without thinking, that doing what comes naturally is the key to survival. Many people seem to lose that key along with childhood innocence. Actually, they don't lose it. They just forget to use it.

Albert Einstein said that we humans can do whatever we like except choose what we like to do. This is preprogrammed into our brains at birth. As we mature, the biocomputer's thinking function kicks in and we develop the power to reason along with an urge to figure things out. Some people use their reasoning powers to figure out how things should be. This, of course, presumes that things are not perfect exactly the way they are. It is the belief that they live in an imperfect world that tends to make believers mistrust their feelings. So they squelch their natural inclinations, intuitive tendencies, and creative urges as part of a trade-off. The well-being that comes with doing what they feel like doing is sacrificed for the sense of security and moral rectitude they get by making themselves do what they think they should do or what they think other people think they should do.

The urge to do what we feel like doing when we feel like doing it is, like any other urge, an energy surge. A ripple in the field of consciousness. You can't reason with it any more than you can with a head of steam.

It can be directed, but trying to squelch it or ignore it is dangerous. Unless it is vented and allowed to express itself from time to time, it builds up to the point of explosion.

We worked with a corporate CEO whose no-nonsense, nose-to-the-grindstone attitude helped him build a successful business that made lots of money. Except for a tendency to throw temper tantrums, he thought he was doing pretty well. When it came to his attention that these outbursts were alienating his employees and threatening to disrupt his marriage, he decided to control them the way he controlled everything else in his life. Any time he felt the urge to rant and rave because things were not going exactly the way he thought they should, he simply stifled it. Then, he spiraled down into a deep depression for which he had to be hospitalized to make sure he wouldn't kill himself.

In the hospital, doctors learned that he was an art school graduate who had always had a passion for painting. As a young man, he had decided to believe that money was the key to survival and that willingness to sacrifice and work hard was the price he would have to pay for financial security. So he sacrificed his creativity, took a job at a television station, worked hard, climbed the corporate ladder, and finally made enough money to buy the company. He said he still felt the urge to paint but squelched it because he believed that doing what you like to do just because it makes you feel good is a waste of time since it does not produce income. So they put him in an art therapy program. As soon as he got back to painting full-time, his depression disappeared. A few weeks later, he said he was feeling happier than he had in decades. After that, he was discharged on antidepressant drugs, which were supposed to keep him functioning. They didn't.

After he got home, he went right back to his old ways. Running the business and thinking about it took up all his waking hours. So painting got pushed onto a back burner and, finally, off the stove altogether. He got more and more irritable, and over the next eighteen months, again went through the exact same scenario, which ended with his being admitted to the hospital in a suicidal depression, which cleared completely in art therapy class. After going through a third cycle, he consulted us on the advice of a friend.

As he was telling us his story, he had a sudden flash of insight. It struck him that setting aside two or three hours every day to vent his urge to paint would be much more cost effective than spending a month or two in the sanatorium every couple of years. The businessman and the creative artist in him agreed to a win-win arrangement that worked a lot better than antidepressant drugs, which the psychiatrist agreed to allow him to discontinue as long as he promised to keep on painting.

What changed this man's life was a paradigm shift. He dumped the belief that doing something you feel like doing just because you feel like doing it is self-indulgent, a waste of time, and without value. Along with the belief, he dumped a pack of troubles.

In the last quarter of the twentieth century, a belief

that has been floating around in the human psyche re-surfaced at the cutting edge of modern scientific thought. James Lovelock, who used to be a consultant engineer for NASA's jet propulsion laboratory, decided that his research data would make more sense if planet Earth was a living organism. His flash of insight came to be known as the "Gaia hypothesis." Gaia is the name of an ancient goddess now known as Mother Earth or Mother Nature. In the old days, people pictured her as having human form. Recently, photos taken by NASA astronauts picture her as a blue and white ball hanging out in space for those of us who would like to feel nur-tured and cared for by some higher power but who can't quite get themselves to believe in God. Even for those who can, Lovelock's theory is worth considering.

There is a story about a spiritual seeker who walks up to a pizza stand and says, "Make me one with every-thing." The Gaia hypothesis can do this for you. You don't have to swallow it whole. Just allow that it might be true and remember that the key question is, "Will believing that it might be true make my life work better?"

The theory can also serve those who feel a need to find meaning and purpose in their lives. It implies that each of us is a single cell in a living body. Just as your body takes care of and nurtures each of its cells, Gaia cares for and nurtures each of us. In return for that care, every cell has a job it is supposed to do for the benefit of the larger body. Those who do what they are supposed to do find that their daily needs are always met. We would like to suggest that what you feel like doing, from moment to moment, is what you are supposed to be doing. Merlin Stone, author of a well-received book about ancient goddesses, says that doing whatever she feels like doing whenever she feels like doing it makes her life work really well.

"I always know what I'm supposed to do next because I get excited about it. When my body is filled with excitement and energy—'this feels good; this is fun'—that is the goddess (Gaia) telling me what she wants me to do. You might think if you followed that way of living, you would never get anything practical done. Like shopping or washing the floor. But I'm always amazed, because invariably, there will always be that moment when I actually feel like shopping or actually feel like washing the floor. So in the long run, everything gets done and gets done the way it ought to. I have this wonderful sense of swimming along with the flow and everything I ever need just keeps appearing along my path."

There is a children's game in which one player hides an object and guides the others to it by saying "hot" when they are getting close and "cold" when they are wandering off. Gaia guides us the same way, except instead of words, she uses feelings. Pleasure for hot, pain for cold. When we say pleasure, we are talking about how it feels while emptying a very full bladder after a very long wait. This kind of feeling is how Mother Nature rewards living creatures for doing what we are supposed to do for our own good. Getting in touch with what is fun for you to do puts you in touch with what Gaia needs you to do. If you neglect this need because you have no time for it or because you think something else is more important, Gaia will show you her dark side.

Rolling Thunder, a Native American medicine man, puts it this way, "Everyone in this life has something they are supposed to do. If you don't do what you're supposed to do, you have terrible bad luck."

This next story makes what Rolling Thunder said crystal clear.

One day, farmer Zeek decided it was time to "git him a wife." He was making good money, and he needed someone to cook, clean, and do chores and all the things a wife is supposed to do for a man. So he bought an ad in a big city newspaper and ran it for a week. When he got an answer and a photograph from a likely looking woman named Zelda, he sent her a train ticket and arranged for the preacher to meet and marry them at the station.

On the morning of the big day, Zeek hitched Nellie, his favorite horse, to the wagon and drove into town. When they got there, Nellie took an instant dislike to Zelda and during the ceremony bit her. Looking Nellie in the eye, Zelda calmly said. "That's one." On the way home, Zeek let Zelda take the reins. Nellie didn't like this, so she bucked and reared until Zeek took them back. As she handed Zeek the reins, Zelda looked at Nellie and said, "That's two." Back at the farm, as Zelda was stepping down from the wagon, Nellie lurched forward and sent her sprawling in the dust. Pulling a pistol from her purse, Zelda said, "That's three," and shot the horse dead. Zeek flew into a rage. He called Zelda vile names and threatened to horsewhip her. The sight of the smoking gun brought him up short. Zelda brushed herself off, looked Zeek in the eye, and calmly said, "That's one."

If Zelda represents Gaia, Nellie would be the part of us that resists doing what we are supposed to do to serve her. Gaia herself doesn't carry a gun. Her weapons are what Shakespeare's Hamlet called "the slings and arrows of outrageous fortune" or what Rolling Thunder calls "terrible bad luck."

Gaia is by nature forgiving. She doesn't hold a grudge. If you pay attention to her early warnings and clean up your act before the count of three, you and she will get along just fine and everything will be okay. If not, you will probably get recycled. It is that simple. It is important to remember that if you want to stay on Gaia's good side, feeling good and having fun is the name of the game. If you are doing poorly on that score, you need to look at the possibility that you are coming down with a case of pleasure deficiency syndrome.

Maia was an attorney from a tiny country in Africa. She had been over here for about a year working for an advanced degree in public administration. She called to ask if we could help her cope with joint pains, headaches, constant fatigue, and inability to conceive. Doctors back home and at the university health service had conducted all kinds of tests but couldn't find a physical reason for her troubles. They all said her symptoms were probably caused by stress. That diagnosis distressed her even more.

"My government paid for my husband and me to come over here and learn some skills we could use to serve our people. They are also paying for tuition, books, and living expenses. We are not a rich country. I carry a heavy course load because I want to get through quickly and keep expenses down. English is not my first language, so I have to work even harder just to keep up. And yet, it seems, the harder I work, the behinder I get. Now, to make things worse, I have to put up with all this pain and exhaustion. The doctors gave me pills. When I take them, the hurting stops, but I get so groggy I have even more trouble concentrating. If I fall any further behind in my work, I'll have to drop out and go home in disgrace. I can't bear to think about that. It makes me too sad."

Maia was at the end of her rope. And it was slipping through her fingers. As it turned out, she could have let go then and there and it wouldn't have mattered. What did matter was the hurting. Letting go just a little might ease the pain, so we asked what she was doing for fun these days. She said having fun wasn't high on her list of priorities. Actually, it wasn't on it at all.

"I have no time for frivolity," was how she put it. "I barely have time for food. While I'm eating, I read. Every time I go to the bathroom, I make sure to take a textbook along. Sometimes I'm in there eating, reading, and relieving myself all at the same time. If I wasn't feeling so bad, I'd think it was comical."

Maia was well aware of what was ailing her. She could even call it by name—migratory arthritis aggravated by stress. Knowing that didn't make her feel any better. When identifying the cause doesn't lead to a cure, it is a good idea to try another approach. We decided to pursue Parsifal's second question: What purpose does it serve?

Working on the theory that life experience is a hologram projected by the brain and programmed by belief, we would guess that the purpose of Maia's ailments was to get her to discard dysfunctional beliefs. The most obvious being the notion that through self-denial and hard work, she could save money. Debunking that one was easy. When she checked her records and added up the amount of money she had spent over the past year on professional fees, lab tests, drugs, and transportation to and from various doctors' offices, it turned out to be significantly more than what it would have cost her in living expenses to carry half the course load she was currently carrying and to spend another year learning the same skills at a more relaxed rate.

A second misconception she had to give up was the belief that hard work never killed anybody. That myth exploded for her when she read an article on a condition the Japanese call "death from overwork." In 1989, the report said, the condition claimed thirty-five thousand lives in Japan. The victims' work habits were remarkably similar to Maia's. Fifteen hours a day with no days off or vacation time. Some keeled over in their offices or at their work stations without having seen their families for weeks or even months. Maia hadn't seen her parents for a year. That got us talking about pleasure deficiency syndrome and about the core belief at the root of her problems.

Maia's secondary education was in a Catholic mission school. The nuns taught her to speak French and to believe self-indulgence was a sin. To her mind, it was right up there with the original one. The other side of the coin was the belief that service to others is the highest good. We used the second belief as a lever to pry her loose from the first. To show how self-sacrifice to the point of burnout is counterproductive, we posed a hypothetical question.

"Suppose you are in a life-and-death situation requiring immediate medical intervention. In the emergency room, two doctors are on duty. The first has been working fifteen hours a day seven days a week while the other just vacationed in Hawaii. It is the second one's first day back on the job. Today is the day they switch. Both are equally well trained and competent. You get to choose which one will handle your case. Would you have a preference?"

Maia had to admit that to serve others effectively, she had to begin by taking care of herself. Also, that practicing self-denial and dedicating her life to serving others so she could get in good with God was a perverse form of self-indulgence. The lawyer in her acknowledged the validity of the argument and conceded the issue.

The little kid in her was ecstatic. It made her eyes shine. Then, she realized her joints weren't hurting. Another part of her, a relationship-oriented, feminine aspect, felt badly about throwing in the towel and letting her people down, until we pointed out that by nurturing her own inner child she might be more likely to create a child within her. She thought she should at least complete the last two months of the spring term and then consider her options.

To do this, she had to be rid of her symptoms. Since they were manifestations of acute pleasure deficiency, removing them would require a vigorous program of affirmative action—active pursuit of pleasure. The problem was, she had forgotten how to have fun. We asked her what she used to love to do before the nuns talked her into believing pleasure was sinful. She said she enjoyed listening to music, dancing, and playing with young children and animals. Maia thought she would probably still enjoy those things but couldn't see any way to fit them into an already impossible schedule.

This is a common complaint these days. People get so involved in getting things done and accomplishing goals that they forget to take the time to relax and unwind. Maybe that is what happened to those people in Japan. Maybe they developed fatal cases of pleasure deficiency syndrome. To paraphrase an old American proverb: All work and no play makes Jack a dead boy.

Think about how hard your heart works. Twenty-four hours a day, year in, year out. How does it do that without burning out? Simple. After each stroke of work, it relaxes completely. Imagine what would happen if it decided it couldn't take the time to relax and refill because its work is too important.

Maia's belief that she could work nonstop and be

perfectly well would have had Zelda hollering, "That's one." There was still plenty of time to clean up her act. When she came in for her next session, she said she had figured out a way to get her brain to work as effectively as her heart does. She bought a portable cassette player with headphones, a batch of enjoyable music tapes, thirty minutes to a side, and a wristwatch with a silent alarm that taps you on the wrist when it goes off. During the ten hours she spent in the library after class every day, she set it to go off every ninety minutes. When it did, she closed her book or turned off the computer, put on the earphones, and listened to one side of one tape. When it was finished, she reset the alarm and went back to work. After some negotiation, she reluctantly agreed that when she got home at 11 P.M., instead of burying her nose in a book, she would immerse her body in a bubble bath, turn off the world for the time it takes to play one side of one tape, and then go to bed. Her determination to get well was strong enough to allow her to run the risk of spending her Sundays hanging out with friends, going to dances, and visiting with her three-year-old nephew and his little puppy dog. She half expected that at any moment God would strike her dead.

God didn't. Instead, Gaia forgave her. After six weeks on this regime, she was free of pain, and her ability to concentrate increased geometrically. She got much more done with much less effort and got through the rest of the semester in good shape. Then, she took a quantum leap.

Operating out of her old belief system, she had arranged

to carry another heavy course load in summer session and to plow through the rest of the year without coming up for air. One evening, in a bubble bath, it struck her that she had a choice. Instead of automatically doing what other people (the government officials who sent her here and the nuns who taught her how to speak and what to think) thought she should be doing, she could, for the first time in her life, consider doing what she felt like doing: taking a break and spending the summer back home with her family. The very thought of doing that sent a surge of energy tingling through her body. She wasn't sure whether it was panic, joy, or a combination of both. We told her it was a charge of raw energy coming out of the explosion of her old belief systems—an adrenaline rush.

"Whatever you decide to call it is what it is for you," we told her. "Better to use it productively rather than worry about what to name it."

As long as she thought of her agitated state as joy or pure energy, Maia could deal with it. She used it to cancel her summer classes and book passage home. While she was there, a revolution overthrew the government that had sent her to school and, with it, any chance she might have had of serving her people as a public administrator. This was fine with Maia because the main thing she had learned at the university was that she hated bureaucracy. Now, she would have to settle for practicing law, living close to her family, and doing whatever she felt like doing whenever she felt like doing it. Not a bad deal, actually. We received a birth announcement from Maia and her husband about a year later. They are the proud parents of a healthy baby girl.

Maia raised her life game score from minus seven to plus nine by dumping a few old beliefs and picking up some new ones. The old beliefs programmed her bio-computer to print out a physical condition that was living proof that computer programmers are right when they say, "Garbage in, garbage out." The notion that physical conditions and even physical bodies themselves are perceptions that can be reprogrammed by altering mental software (thoughts and images) could eventually displace some widely held and well-entrenched beliefs about what we need to be doing to be well, happy, and successful.

6

Finding Your Way

The authorities of the universe
put you here with some tasks
strictly appointed you in your constitution
and so long as you work at that,
you are well and successful.
RALPH WALDO EMERSON

Once upon a time, there was a school in the forest where all creatures came to learn how to do their best. Many students had to stay after school to go over things they were having trouble learning. Eagle had to practice swimming. Squirrel had to try over and over again to soar. Turtle had to master tree climbing. It seems laughable when we imagine the animals in this story trying to develop skills for which they have no natural ability. How many of us are spending our lives doing the same sort of things?

We humans are routinely taught to pursue goals and engage in careers requiring skills that have nothing to do with our natural inclinations and intuitive tendencies. Each of us has special talents, abilities, and interests. These vary a great deal from one person to the next. What is more, one person's pleasure can be another's torture. The first step on the road to success is to recognize our special talents and unique abilities—the things that give us pleasure while we are doing them. What, for you, seems like it might be interesting, engrossing, or fun to do?

It is not unusual for people to draw a blank when first asked this question. Many of our clients at the Transformational Learning Center realize they have become so "adulterated" and out of touch with the natural child they used to be that they must, like a newborn baby, rediscover what they love to do. As with any unfoldment, the first few steps are the most unsure and require the most intention and attention. So let's walk through the beginning of the exploration together. Imagine yourself doing each of the following and notice which ones seem appealing:

- Taking a pen and pencil to a beautiful place and sketching what you see.
- Getting a house plant and tending it lovingly.
- Writing a poem, a play, a short story, or perhaps some correspondence.
- Going hiking, finding yourself surrounded by nature.
- Getting a pet to care for, or, if you have pets, training or breeding animals.
- Traveling to new places—even in your own hometown.
- Learning to play a sport you have always been fascinated by.
- Growing food crops. You can start with herb pots in the kitchen window.
- Learning a craft you have always admired for its beauty or utility.

- Learning to play a musical instrument, one whose sound makes you feel wonderful.
- Visiting elderly folks to give them love and to learn from them.
- Flying a kite, maybe even making your own.
- Getting a book that will teach you something you have always wanted to learn more about.
- Starting or joining a group to pursue an interest that has always been near and dear to you (theater, museum, county fair, church).
- Taking a stroll through your favorite area, city or country. Notice what catches your eye.
- Thinking back to what fascinated you as a youngster. That is what you are supposed to get involved in.

Now that you have an idea about what you would like to explore, the next step is to fit this new pursuit into your daily life—TODAY. This may require nothing but a phone call or a half hour actually spent living what you have imagined. Try it. See how you feel about yourself. The results are immediate. Satisfaction, well-being, and a sense of being taken care of (by yourself!). We worked with a client at TLC who had multiple physical complaints. She learned that when she flew a kite she noticed marked improvement of a painful knee condition. She also discovered that allowing herself prolonged periods of peace and quiet in her own home alleviated a digestive disorder. Symptomatic improvement of these two conditions was objectively confirmed by her family doctor, who had already tried everything she could think of to help the woman.

You don't have to get sick as an excuse for allowing yourself to do what you love to do. Over the years, we've seen dramatic positive changes happen for healthy people who learn what they love to do and do it. People who, as Joseph Campbell put it, follow their bliss. For some, this path has led to a new career or to a new relationship.

One man came to us feeling as if his life were over at the age of fifty-two. His significant other ran his affairs and made all the decisions. He was feeling empty, lost, and defeated. During the time we worked with him, he started exploring his talents. He had always been drawn to art exhibits and museums—especially to paintings. We encouraged him to start sketching and painting. He was amazed to see what he could do. This led him to believe that maybe he did have some artistic talent. So, when it came time to redo the kitchen, he sketched ideas and plans. He even got involved in some of the finish work, applying his artistic talents and abilities. As a result, his life partner's attitude toward him improved radically. This was an unexpected and welcome bonus. He accomplished all this by finding out what he loved to do and heading in that direction one step at a time. Wonderful things happen for people who allow themselves the luxury of getting involved in activities that feed them back.

Why not take the leap now? Set aside a little time each day to develop some of the wonderfulness that is waiting there inside you. Give yourself a little push by picturing yourself doing what you love to do on a regular basis. Notice how good this feels. Then, do it.

All that is required is that you spend some time each day doing something you really love to do. It can be a different activity each day. The only rule is that it be fun for you while you are doing it—the kind of fun kids are having when they are totally involved in an activity and beaming with joy.

For some of you, cuddling your cat will work. For others, a walk on the beach or in the park might be a real "treat." It is refreshing, exhilarating, and while you are doing it you feel absolutely blissful.

The key is to "treat" yourself DAILY. Make "treat times" as important as mealtimes. Maybe even set aside a certain time of day and faithfully "treat" yourself then—the way people do when they take coffee breaks at the office.

If you do this for two weeks without fail, you will have created a delicious new habit that might improve your health and certainly will improve your disposition. You may also be surprised to find that you are more clearheaded and efficient while taking care of your daily responsibilities if you allow the child within you to have these "treat" times every day. Like the proverbial apple a day, they keep the doctor away.

7

Mind Medicine

Your symptoms may not be in your head,
but the power to get rid of them may well be.
STUART BERGER, M.D.

The desk clerk at a posh hotel looked up to see an elegant matron waiting to register. Her uniformed chauffeur, carrying a young man, was standing beside her. Without batting an eye, the clerk apologized because the hotel had no facilities for the handicapped. The matron wanted to know who was handicapped.

"Your son," answered the clerk. "Apparently he isn't able to walk."

The matron smiled and said, "He can walk just fine. But, thank God, he doesn't have to."

Think of mama as an insurance company, the chauffeur as the medical profession, and the young man as the patient who expects doctors to do for him what he is perfectly capable of doing for himself while someone else foots the bill, and you'll understand the root of our current health-care crisis. Here is another way of looking at the same sort of thinking.

Brenda and Bert took their new car out for a spin in the country and a picnic by a lake. When it was time to leave, they noticed that they had locked the keys inside.

"Not to worry," said Bert. "Help is just a phone call away. Our car insurance includes road service." As he walked toward the telephone, Brenda called after him, "Tell them to hurry, dearie. It's starting to rain and we left the top down."

The main problem with this "Let George do it" approach is that it is very expensive. Also, it leads to arguments. In 1989, 85 percent of labor disputes were caused by squabbles over who was going to pay for astronomically high and rapidly rising health insurance premiums. That same year, insurance companies said they were having trouble keeping up with the cost of a health-care delivery system that the surgeon general of the United States had described as in a state of crisis and in danger of breaking down.

Dr. John Knowles, former secretary of health, education, and welfare, pointed to a way out of this mess. He told his colleagues that the next major event in medicine will not be the discovery of powerful new drugs or the invention of exotic new therapies but "what patients can learn to do for themselves."

Dealing with minor aches, pains, and run-of-the-mill maladies is about as hard as getting into a locked convertible when the top is down. Some people aren't aware of this. Those who are don't get hooked on expensive, industrial-strength over-the-counter remedies. When you get right down to it, they may all be placebos, about as effective as the old-time snake oil remedies. That is not to say they don't work. Often, they do. The word "maximum strength" on the outside of the package may have as much to do with this as the stuff on the inside. The active ingredient, the one that does the job, is not in the package but in the patient. It can be found in all humans.

There once was a guru who could cure anything. To get to see him, patients had to trek into the interior of Tibet, climb an enormous mountain, and camp outside his cave for three days and three nights. Then, the guru would come out, chant a short prayer, and tell them to go home because they were healed. It worked every time. Whoever came went home healthy no matter what they had.

A disciple asked for the secret of his success, and the guru said that if the desire to get well was strong enough to make patients undertake a journey like that and if their faith in his ability was powerful enough to make them spend three days and three nights camped out in this kind of climate, there was nothing more he had to do. By the time he got to see them, they were healed. They expected him to do something, so he chanted.

It's possible that Lourdes and other religious shrines operate on the same principle. People make the pilgrimage, put their faith in some higher power, and their faith makes them whole. Dr. Albert Schweitzer believed that the rituals performed by African witch doctors in the jungle activated what he called "the doctor within," which generated healing from the inside out. Today, we call this the immune defense system. Whatever we call it, there obviously is a powerful healing mechanism inherent in every human. Intention, faith, and ritual seem to trigger it.

A recent study of twenty-three hundred people over

sixty-four years of age has concluded that those who think of their health as "excellent" are four to five times more likely to live four more years than those who think of their health as "poor," even if the participants are actually equally healthy. According to the *New York Times*, five other large studies involving a total of twenty-three thousand people reached similar conclusions. We are just beginning to understand how this works.

A case history demonstrates this connection between state of health and state of mind. Lizzy came to see us because the doctor found a suspicious shadow on her chest X ray and thought it might be malignant. He wanted to put her into the hospital for a biopsy, and she said in all her seventy-six years she had never been in one of those places and she wasn't about to start now. The doctor said the sooner she came to her senses and let him do what had to be done, the better. He advised her to go home and think about it. Lizzy went to church instead and found what she was looking for.

"I was on my knees in the empty church, praying for salvation and guidance when as clearly as I see you, I saw Jesus. I asked him to help me. He smiled and put his hand on my chest. It felt like it was on fire. Then, he told me to rise up and be on my way because my faith had made me whole.

"I know I'm completely healed. The problem is Dr. John. He doesn't believe it. He said what I had in the church was a hallucination and hallucinations can't cure cancer. He said I need to face reality and submit to surgery. How could I? That would be a breach of faith.

"Science is his religion. I respect that. I just wish he could be less dogmatic and respect mine, too. I've known him since he was a toddler and don't want him to be mad at me. That's why I'm here. Could you maybe call him and set things right between us?"

Dr. John said Lizzy was special to him, and he couldn't just stand by and watch her die. He also knew she wasn't about to follow his advice no matter how mad he got. He sounded really frustrated.

"All things considered," Dr. Oyle suggested. "We think visual imagery might work."

He was skeptical. "I'll believe that when I see a normal X ray. I'm not so sure I'd believe it even then, but no way is she going to do what I tell her, so I might as well go along with it. Have her call my office and we'll set up a schedule for regular checkups. Maybe I can still get her to change her mind."

Lizzy was delighted. As far as she was concerned, she was healed, but if "disappearing" that shadow on the X ray would make Dr. John happy she was more than willing to try. "He showed it to me. It looks like some kind of fuzzy creature floating on a dark lake. He says it's vicious and if I don't let him destroy it, it will kill me for sure. I know it's dead. The fire in the church did that. I suppose now, it's just a matter of disposing of the body."

To do that, she chose to picture two meat-eating piranha fish and a dolphin swimming together. Solly, Dolly, and Polly. She pictured them playing catch with the fuzzy ball. Solly took a bite and tossed it to Polly, who took another bite and flipped it over to Dolly, who tore off a piece and tossed it back to Solly. The game was fun and the fuzzy ball got smaller and smaller till it was gone. Then, she imagined them cruising through her bloodstream hunting down and devouring any other little fuzzies that might have escaped the fire. Three times a day, for fifteen minutes, she sat with her eyes closed, picturing this scenario. This done, she offered a prayer of thanksgiving and went about her business.

A friend of Lizzy's said he read a report that people who are told they only have six months to live, believe it, and live as though each day might be their last, tend to have a higher recovery rate from life-threatening illnesses than people who panic and resort to medical heroics. So Lizzy signed up for swimming lessons and a belly dancing class. Three months later, her chest X ray was negative. All it showed was a scar.

The doctor called what happened to Lizzy a "spontaneous remission." Lizzy was sure it was a miracle cure. Calling it a "self-induced spontaneous remission" would make them both right. It's quite possible that Lizzy healed her body with her mind. This method of dealing with disease may be the way out of our current healthcare crisis. Anyone can do it. Faith and an open mind seem to be the key.

When we were teaching at the University of Hawaii School of Public Health, one of our students, a physician from Calcutta, told us about a patient who had a similar experience.

"A farmer came into my clinic with a moderately severe allergic reaction. His body was covered with hives, and he was having some difficulty breathing. I suggested he go into hospital, but he refused so I wrote him a prescription for cortisone tablets. I took great pains to explain that this was very powerful medicine and that he was to take it four times a day without fail. In thirty-six hours, he was back, completely recovered. Very surprising indeed. I asked him what he had done with the remaining medicine. He said there was none because he followed my instructions explicitly. 'I tore your medicine paper into four parts and swallowed one on arising, one with lunch, one with the evening meal, and the last after I was in bed,' he said. He had eaten the paper on which the prescription was written, and he was fully recovered. He requested another medicine paper as insurance against the return of the malady. Naturally, I gave him one."

Allergies and cancers are two examples of what can happen when the body's immune defense system malfunctions. In the first, it overreacts and attacks normal tissues. In the second, it stands idly by and does nothing as malignant cells run wild and ravage the body. Why would it do that? For a long time, we had no idea. Then, a clue turned up in the mental health field. Psychiatrists noticed that people with multiple personalities can be violently allergic when one personality is out and perfectly normal when another is in charge.

Another piece of the puzzle turned up unexpectedly during an experiment carried out by Drs. Ader and Cohen of Rochester University. They wanted to see if they could persuade laboratory rats to turn down an offering of sugar water, which they love. At first, they laced the drinks with a drug that causes nausea. Then, they withdrew the drug and presented the animals with pure sugar water to see if they would associate sweetness with sickness and refuse to drink. (A drug called Antabuse was part of a similar strategy to help humans get unhooked from dependency on alcohol.)

When presented with untainted sugar water in the second half of the experiment, many rats failed to make the connection or just didn't care. They lapped it up. Then, a strange thing happened. They all died. The more they drank or the more concentrated the solution, the sooner they died. A simple sugar water solution was acting like a deadly poison. Autopsies showed immune system destruction.

Checking further, the doctors learned that the drug they were using to produce nausea has a serious side effect. It causes a nonviral form of AIDS. Apparently, the rats had learned to associate the sweet taste of the sugar water not with nausea, but with the toxic side effects of the drug, and to respond with appropriate behavior.

Speculating on the implications of these results, the researchers wrote, "There is no longer any doubt that the mind can control the immune system. At this time (1980), exactly how this happens remains a mystery." With that, a new medical specialty was born. Psychoneuroimmunology (PNI) is the name it goes by. PNI, the study of how the mind, through the brain, controls the immune system, may well be the major advance in medicine predicted by Dr. Knowles—discovery of what patients can learn to do for themselves.

Ader and Cohen's study was a modern version of Pavlov's classic experiment. He taught dogs to salivate at the sound of a bell by ringing it just before feeding them. The animals learned to associate the sound with the food and to respond with appropriate behavior—salivation. This kind of behavior in response to an unrelated stimulus is called a conditioned reflex. Pavlov assumed this happened because new connections were set up in the brain. For him, as for his modern counterparts, exactly how this happened was a mystery. Today, we're happy to say, the mystery has been solved. It is all done with hormones.

In an earlier chapter, we said that a growing number of scientists accept the spiritual principle that observer and observed are one. Applying this principle to the mind-body connection, we believe that mind, the observer, and body, the observed, are more than connected; they are one. You can experience this unity within yourself by trying a simple variation of Pavlov's study. In this experiment, observing scientist and observed subject are one and the same—you yourself.

Picture a ripe yellow lemon on a cutting board. Beside it is a sharp knife. Imagine cutting the lemon into four quarters. See yourself picking up one wedge and put it, juicy side first, into your mouth. Sink your teeth into it and feel the tart juice squirting out of the fruit. Feel it running over the top and sides of your tongue onto the floor of your mouth. Notice any reaction?

Just as the sound of the bell made the dogs salivate, the picture of the lemon in your head made your mouth water. Beliefs are as powerful as mind pictures. In the church, Lizzy saw a vision of Christ and chose to believe it had healing powers. In Calcutta, the farmer chose to believe the same about a prescription for cortisone written on a piece of paper. In each case, the belief made the believer's brain produce the appropriate healing response.

In 1977, Roger Guillemin won a Nobel prize in medicine for demonstrating that the brain is a gland. He showed how it converts thoughts and mental images into chemical messages called hormones, which are injected directly into the bloodstream. Some ten years later, at the National Institute of Mental Health, Candace Pert put the last piece in the mind-body puzzle when she proved that our defender cells have antennae that are tuned to pick up chemical messages emitted from the brain. Like communications from headquarters, these hormones tell individual cells exactly what they're supposed to do.

Lizzy's healing vision was converted into powerful medicines that fired up her killer lymphocytes along with other immune defense units and ordered them into battle. The faith of the farmer in the healing power of the magical medicine paper was translated into chemical compounds that tranquilized his immune system and relieved his allergies. This kind of clinical and experimental evidence should put to rest, once and for all, the worn-out superstition that your mind can't heal your body. IF YOU PUT YOUR MIND TO IT, GETTING THE BODY TO HEAL IS AS EASY AS GETTING OUT OF BED.

If you had to decide which nerves to fire, which muscles to contract, which to relax and when, as well as try to figure out how deeply and how fast you should be breathing while setting your heart rate at the proper level to provide the correct oxygen and fuel mixture to your muscles so they could instantly go from a resting phase to full activity, you'd be several years getting from bed to the bathroom or wherever it is you go when you first get up. Lucky for all of us, that's not necessary. We just decide it's time to get up and the body throws the covers off, gets out of bed, washes, and dresses itself. We don't do that. The body does, automatically. By magic. Here's a little poem to help you see the miracle through the eyes of a child.

I have ten little fingers, and they all belong to me.
I can make them do things. Would you like to see?
I can shut them up tight. I can open them wide.
I can make them stand high. I can make them bend low.
I can wiggle them around, and I can hold them just so.

How do you suppose she does that? By the time we're all grown-up and fully "adulterated," we take this kind of magic for granted. Even worse, we set limits on it. Take the myth of the involuntary nervous system— the belief that things happen in our bodies that are beyond our control, things like heart rate, blood pressure, pain, or the healing process. If you choose to believe that

93

any bodily process is beyond your control, then for you it is. In light of the evidence we have discussed so far, you can choose to believe these processes aren't involuntary— just automatic, yet responsive to your instructions.

A client told us she walked barefoot across an open fire pit without getting burned. According to her, it's just a matter of getting into the right frame of mind. "I heard about people in India doing stuff like that," she said, "but I never thought it had anything to do with me. I figured those people were just a different breed of human being. Then, on the TV, I saw a butcher from Trenton, New Jersey, walk on fire, and it dawned on me that if he could do it, I could, too. He told the reporter it enhanced his self-confidence and made him feel as if he could do anything. That sounded pretty good to me. A couple of days later, I saw an article in the local paper about a lecture demonstration on the art of firewalking. So I went and learned the two most important rules: (1) Stay calm. (2) Direct your thoughts.

"So I just did that, and before I knew it, I was across the hot coals.

"Now, when life gets scary, I follow the same rules. Instead of worrying and making up disaster scenarios about what might happen, I make myself think about the best possible outcome to the situation and you know what? It always comes out that way. I guess that's the bottom line: ALWAYS THINK ABOUT WHAT YOU DO WANT, NEVER WHAT YOU DON'T WANT."

They say a picture is worth a thousand words. So for programming personal experiences, positive imaging should work even better than positive thinking. A good example is a psychologist who set fire to an alcohol-soaked cotton ball in the palm of her hand. After watching it burn for a moment, she closed her fingers over it and snuffed it out.

"In my mind," she said, "I picture my hand encased in a sheet of ice. I can actually feel the freezing cold. Then, I light the fire and imagine it burning on the surface of the ice rather than on my skin. It takes practice, so I wouldn't advise anyone to try this without some preliminary instruction." She went on to say that the purpose of her performance was more than mere theatrics. It was designed to demonstrate that fear of fire is what makes it dangerous. "Once they get past fear, anyone can do what I did. A specific remedy for fear is faith— faith in yourself and the power of your own mind."

We asked her what made her start playing with fire and she said it was an accident. "I was researching visual imagery as a tool for controlling pain and enhancing healing. I read somewhere that the body can't tell the difference between a vivid visual image and an actual experience. You know, like when you dream you're walking, running, or falling, your body feels as if you actually are. Well, let me tell you, I got a chance to verify this for myself first hand. I was pouring a cup of freshly brewed coffee and didn't notice that I was holding the cup upside down. Next thing I knew, scalding hot liquid was splashing off the bottom of the cup all over my hand. I remembered that visual images instruct the brain and, quick as a flash, as soon as I felt the wetness and before the burning sensation hit, I pictured my hand being submerged up to the wrist in a bucket of ice water. I imagined the excess heat being drawn out through my fingertips. I could feel it happening. In my mind's eye, I looked at my hand and saw the skin staying perfectly pink and normal. I held this image in my mind, and an hour after the incident there was no reaction except for some slight redness. The next morning, even that was gone. It struck me that the same technique might work as well before the burn happened and that's what got me started."

We're not suggesting you should learn to walk on fire or hold it in the palm of your hand—just that it's possible. And that it's also possible, if you put your mind to it, to handle heartburn, hives, headaches, or whatever else might ail you. A retired engineer we were working with protected himself from the side effects of radiation therapy. He was being treated for prostate cancer and was told to expect problems with his bladder and lower bowel.

"There is no way we can shield those organs from the X-ray beam," the doctor said, "so they always get a little burned. How bad the symptoms are varies from person to person."

At first, the patient was depressed. When we told him about the psychologist and the cotton ball, he lit up like a Christmas tree. "If she can handle a ball of fire without getting burned, I guess I can handle a beam of X rays," he said. "It's certainly worth a try." Being an engineer, he insisted on familiarizing himself with his anatomy and designing an imaginary protective lead shield. Just before each treatment, he mentally installed it in between the organs to be protected and the area to be irradiated. Several weeks and some twenty-five treatments later, he had zero symptoms. He never did develop any. The radiologist was impressed. He'd heard this kind of thing was possible, but this was the first time he had ever seen it happen.

In ancient Greece, physicians talked about finding a panacea—a medicine that could cure anything. Ideally, such a medicine would be effective, inexpensive, and free of side effects. Our brains secrete just such substances. Enkephalins (that's Greek for "substances in the head") are medicines secreted by the brain in response to thoughts and mind pictures. For simplicity's sake, let's call them "mind medicines." Mind medicines are safe and effective, and seem to have the power to make people feel better no matter what they've got. What's more, they are fast acting and free.

During the lunch break at one of our seminars, a woman drank too much coffee and came back with terrible heartburn. The first step in treating this kind of distress is to turn the symptom into a mental image, to describe it in terms a five-year-old child would understand. We asked the woman with the heartburn to do this, and she said it felt like her belly was on fire. Flames were coming from a base about three inches in diameter in the pit of her stomach and leaping all the way up into her throat. The second step involves making a picture that represents healing, so we asked her how she would put the fire out. She imagined soaking it with ice water sprayed from a high-pressure hose. As the imaginary flames fizzled out, so did the heartburn. Then, the woman let out a loud burp and laughed. She said she half expected to see smoke coming out of her mouth.

As he was coming back into the building after the same break, a young man tripped and banged his knee on a concrete step. He hit it hard, and it really hurt. Converting the pain into an image, he said it felt like there was a wooden ball about the size of a walnut jammed under his kneecap. To get rid of it, he pictured it bursting into flame and going up in smoke. In less time than it takes to tell, the ball was gone and so was the pain.

As we said, getting yourself to heal is as easy as getting out of bed. Tell your body what you want it to do, and it responds. The best way to do this is to make a clear picture of what you want. The simpler and more childlike the picture, the better the results. Skepticism and disbelief inhibit the process, so adopt a scientific attitude, keep an open mind, and watch what happens.

Pick a symptom—any symptom you believe might be relieved by something you can buy in a drugstore. Next time it troubles you, before taking the drug, try making an image—a simple picture of what it feels like. A tight muscle might feel like a knotted rope. A stuffy nose might suggest a tube jammed full of cotton. Once you've got the image clearly in your mind, change it and watch what happens to the symptom. See the knot coming loose, and the muscle relaxes. Imagine the cotton wads disappearing, and the nose clears.

If expectations create personal reality, there is every reason to believe that watching for improvement makes it happen. Try it. You'll like it. Think of all the time, money, and energy you can save not having to buy expensive over-the-counter remedies to deal with run-of-the-mill aches and pains. Remember that visual imagery is not to replace competent medical care. Nevertheless, even in more serious cases, it has a definite place supplementing and amplifying the effectiveness of any medicine and/or treatment.

Many people who live in big cities wheeze. Following the doctrine of specificity, we would say that the specific cause for the wheezing is muscle spasm and accumulating mucus in the breathing tubes. This would lead traditional doctors to prescribe drugs that relax the muscles and clear the passages. Statistics on the sky-rocketing incidence of asthma in the United States suggest that this increasingly expensive approach is about as effective as using drugs and surgery to reverse coronary artery disease. People who think in terms of purpose would probably move to the country where the air is clean because that's what the wheeze is trying to get them to do. This would require that the wheezer reorder his or her priorities and decide that being well is more important than anything else. Looking at the larger picture, society as a whole could decide to clean up our dirty air. That, interestingly enough, would require a comprehensive life-style change on the part of every American.

A thousand-mile journey starts with a single step. So

if you are not ready to change your address and would like to experiment with a less radical form of life change, you might consider this approach that worked well for Susan. Here she tells it in her own words.

"I had always been the nonathlete until I decided to take up walking. Actually, my body told me to. One look in the mirror and the message was clear.

"I was really determined to change. On the kitchen calendar, I marked how long I walked each day. At first, it was only ten or fifteen minutes five days a week. I usually walked early in the day, just to get it over with. For the first six months, I had to force myself out the door most of the time.

"Then, things started changing. After a walk, for the rest of the day, I felt calmer, satisfied. I tried running some affirmations through my head while I was walking to amp the feeling. It worked. I would think phrases like these to the beat of my footsteps:

I am healthy.
I am lean.
I am light.
I am graceful.

"In time, my walks were averaging thirty minutes and I would feel a warm glow when I got home. Then, one day, as I was rolling out of bed, I glanced down and actually saw the vague outlines of muscles on the fronts and sides of my thighs. That was it. I had BELIEVED this would work and now I could SEE the result.

"Walking became a high point of the day—head up,

body straight, moving at a good clip and running positive thoughts through my head. I'd play with them, trying different combinations. As I look back, that was the beginning of my writing career!

"Now, years later, my body insists on its daily walk. I'm in better shape. My posture is better. I feel stronger. And the changes have spilled over into every part of my life. My stamina, both mental and physical, is increasing, I am more clearheaded and aware—especially of the weather, since walking at the coast means watching for the breaks between storms. I started out getting my satisfaction from the minutes totaled on the kitchen calendar. Now, my satisfaction comes from within.

"Before taking up walking, I would think I was just getting nervous whenever I felt an energy surge in my body. Now, I use that energy. Then, I get to sit back and enjoy the glow."

8

The Doctor Within

Healing comes only from that which gets
the patient beyond entanglement with the ego.
CARL JUNG

If you take a hundred people with the same disease and have them treated by the same doctor with identical medicines, you'll get what's called a "bell curve" of results. The majority of patients will do about as well as can be expected. Even in this group, some will do better than average, and others not quite as well. At one end of the curve, a few people will make dramatic, rapid recoveries, while at the other end some won't respond at all. Everything else being equal, the factors making the difference must lie within the patient. What we're discussing here is finding out what these factors are and how to make them work for you.

Factor number one is intention. Recovery has to be the patient's prime priority. This is not always the case, especially when it involves radical life change. There are business executives with chest pain who choose to run the risk of heart attack rather than slowing down or retiring. Sometimes we're not even willing to make a little life change. Have you or has anyone you know ever gone to work with a cold or the flu rather than miss a day's pay? Many people go to doctors or other healing practitioners hoping they can fix them and make them

103

well enough to keep working. This is low-grade intention. High-grade intention would be determination to be healthy no matter what it takes.

Factor number two is faith. The healer can be a physician in a state-of-the-art Western hospital or a witch doctor in the African jungle. According to Dr. Albert Schweitzer, each performs a ritual appropriate to his or her culture. The physician administers a treatment to eliminate a disease entity. The witch doctor chants an encantation to exorcise an evil spirit. There is no real difference between a disease entity and an evil spirit. Therefore, the witch doctor and the physician are performing the same service.

In either case, the patient energizes the ritual with faith in the practitioner and the ritual. This activates what Dr. Schweitzer called "the doctor within." The patient then gets an appropriate dose of mind medicines, and healing happens. The clearer the intention, the stronger the faith, and the faster the healing.

Creating mind medicines to relieve symptoms is an important first step toward getting well again, but by itself it's not enough. To stay well, the patient has to discover the message in the symptom and follow through by making the appropriate life change that nothing less than that symptom could get him or her to make. If you sit on a tack, your rear end hurts. For temporary relief you can buy painkillers or secrete them with your brain. That's like pulling the battery out of the smoke alarm while staying in the burning building. For a permanent cure, you have to get out of the building or put the fire out. By the same token, to remove the source of the pain, you have to get up off the tack. A change in how you live is required if you want your body to stop sending you the signal to change.

Question: Why does a chicken cross the road?
Answer: To get to the other side.

A person gets sick for the same reason. For a caterpillar, the other side is a butterfly. We all have the opportunity to see the events in our lives this way at any given moment.

When trying to understand what's happening in the world, looking for a purpose (guidance) makes more sense than hunting for a cause (blame). Maybe we could cope more effectively with disease entities, evil spirits, or whatever it is that makes us sick if we knew what they were trying to tell us or what they were trying to get us to do.

At the University of California School of Medicine in San Francisco, Dr. Dean Ornish devised a clinical study we believe supports that theory. He compared two approaches to coronary artery disease, a leading cause of death in America.

In this disorder, the feeder arteries that nourish the heart get clogged and block blood flow. Chest pains are an early warning sign. As the condition progresses, the heart muscle dies and, if blockage gets bad enough, so does the patient.

The first approach Dr. Ornish tested was "the old way." When treating this or any other disease, Western doctors have religiously followed the doctrine of specificity. That's the basic premise (paradigm) under which today's medical orthodoxy operates. It says each disease has a specific cause that must be removed by a specific remedy. Following this doctrine, traditional researchers determined that blood vessels were being clogged by cholesterol, which sticks to the walls and piles up to narrow the passage. Armed with this information and a test for measuring levels of cholesterol in the bloodstream, they mounted a three-pronged attack on the problem: (1) Cut cholesterol intake by avoiding fatty foods. (2) Take drugs to clear it out of the bloodstream. (3) Replace damaged arteries with new ones. Dr. Ornish had one group of patients follow these guidelines.

And now, dear reader, time for a brief aside. It has been said that every solution creates new problems. This seems to be true about step one of the above approach. A group of British researchers working with monkeys found that artificially lowering the animals' blood cholesterol by cutting fat out of the diet makes them mean. Another group, working in Finland, found this to be true for humans, too. They reported that people who lower blood cholesterol through dietary restriction of fat tend to become irritable, aggressive, and violent. Statistics show these people are more likely to get involved in automobile accidents and heated arguments that lead to injury and death. If a treatment can have such serious side effects, is it worth taking at all? Dr. Ornish's study provides an answer to this question.

He picked fifty people with four or five blocked arteries apiece and divided them into two groups. Group A got specific therapy consisting of drugs and surgery as outlined in the three-step traditional approach. They were also advised to follow dietary recommendations and life-style guidelines put out by the American Heart Association. Patients in Group B got no surgery and took no cholesterol-lowering drugs. Their treatment program, "the new way," focused mainly on making what Dr. Ornish called "comprehensive life-style changes." These people radically altered the way in which they were living. Progress in both groups was monitored by means of a sophisticated device that accurately measures the thickness of deposits in the heart's feeder arteries. At this writing, the study is still going on and Dr. Ornish has published some preliminary results.

In the group relying on drugs and surgery, eleven of the first seventeen patients examined after treatment were worse. Their arteries were more clogged than before. In the life-style change group, ten of twelve showed definite improvement. Here is how Dr. Ornish sums up his findings so far. "People who make comprehensive life-style changes show early reversal of coronary artery disease without taking cholesterol-lowering drugs or undergoing surgery."

If a life-style change reverses a disease process, it stands to reason that the previous one had something to do with precipitating it. Following this line of reasoning, we could say that the disease had a purpose—to force the patient to make necessary therapeutic change.

This represents a radical departure from "the old way," a specific cure for a specific disease.

Dr. Ornish's study poses a direct challenge to the doctrine of specificity. It's not the first to come from within the medical establishment. An earlier challenge came from no less an authority than Dr. Hans Selye. The holder of three doctoral degrees (one in medicine, one in chemistry, and one in philosophy), he won international acclaim for proving that nonspecific stress can initiate, aggravate, and complicate a whole host of diseases previously thought to be unrelated. Picking up on the ancient Greek physicians' dream of finding a panacea, a cure-all, he said he believed we should be able to find a nonspecific remedy to make people feel better no matter what they've got. During the early part of the twentieth century, another famous physician, Dr. Carl Jung, had already hinted at what that remedy might be. In a flat-out rejection of the doctrine of specificity, Dr. Jung wrote, "Healing comes only from that which gets the patient beyond entanglement with the ego."

Some fifty years later, in the course of unraveling a medical mystery, an orthopedic surgeon came up with hard facts that support Dr. Jung's opinion. A number of male patients with active careers were being referred to him because of persistent pain and tenderness in one buttock. Sometimes the pain would shoot down the back of the leg on the affected side, and in severe cases, the leg showed slight signs of shriveling. Careful examination, state-of-the-art X rays, and sophisticated lab tests failed to pinpoint a specific cause.

108

Thinking in terms of purpose rather than cause, we might wonder what the symptoms were telling these guys about how they were living their lives and what changes needed to be made. A key clue was the fact that they all had to take time off from work. Flat on their backs in the hospital or lying around the house in leisure clothing, they got better. Then they went back to work and the symptoms recurred. They had different occupations, so the specific trigger couldn't be what they were doing to earn a living. There must be something else connected with going to work that these patients had in common. But what was it?

Like Archimedes in the bathtub or Newton sitting under the apple tree, the doctor saw the answer and solved the mystery in a flash of insight. Wallets. When he went to work, each patient carried a wallet crammed full of credit, bank, membership, identification, and business cards, which he stuffed into a back pocket of his pants. Then, like a hen on eggs, he sat on them all day. The bulging wallet acted like a tumor that pressed on the sciatic nerve and created the symptoms. Specific treatment of this condition is a noninvasive procedure called walletectomy. Removal of the lump from the rear pocket of the pants. The contents of this clot are all pieces of identification. As such, they serve the ego. Obviously, in these cases at least, Dr. Jung was right.

Ponderous purse syndrome is a similar condition found in women. The symptoms are the same except that pain and tenderness happen in the neck and arm. A physical exam includes weighing the purse slung over one shoulder. Fully loaded it can weigh twelve to fifteen pounds. That's more than enough to compress and irritate the large nerves that run through the neck and shoulder into the arm.

In both sexes, the symptoms send signals that the patient has to lighten his or her load. Since the excess baggage carried in wallets and purses belongs to the ego, that's easier said than done. A surprising number of people couldn't bring themselves to part with the offending object or enough of its contents to make a difference even after they found out what it was doing to their bodies. They just switched it from side to side and hoped for the best.

Apparently, the feminine ego can be a pain in the neck and the masculine ego a pain in the butt. In spite of that, people hang on to it for dear life. Letting go is so scary, mere pain can't pry it loose. What would you do if for reasons of health you were told to give up carrying a wallet or a purse? Or even worse, to sacrifice your career, your present surroundings, or some ingrained habit?

Ego, like a corporation, is an artificial entity invented by the intellect. A collection of habit patterns and survival strategies, it exists only in the mind of the person it inhabits. In healthy people, there are a series of ego entities as they progress through the various stages of their lives. Like a spent fuel tank on a space vehicle, the ego that's appropriate to a specific phase drops away as the person moves from one stage of life into the next. For people who identify with a passing ego and mistake it for who they really are, the thought of ego death can be even more terrifying than the thought of physical death.

Identification with the ego—the belief that what we do is who we are—is widespread in our culture and ingrained in our language. Suppose you're at a party and notice a stranger in the crowd. If you ask someone to tell you who that is, they'll probably respond with a name and an occupation. ("That's Jack. He's a used car salesman." Or, "That's Jane. She's a nuclear physicist.") Can you see yourself as more than what you happen to be doing in this phase of your life? Actually, who you ARE is much more than all the doing you can possibly accomplish in this lifetime.

We worked with an accountant named Sam. He wasn't just another person practicing accounting. Until the day the company gave him a gold watch, a farewell party, and a pension, Sam totally identified with the accountant in him. To his mind, that's who he was. One year after they forced him to retire, Sam was told he had six months to live. A blood test for cancer activity with a normal value of 0 to 1 came back 160. Malignant cells had spread throughout his body and invaded the liver, so it was too late for surgery or radiation.

"The best we can offer you," said the doctor, "is a course of chemotherapy. It will slow the tumor's rate of growth, keep you a bit more comfortable, and buy you a little extra time. But it's not a cure. For that you'd need a miracle."

Sam believed in miracles, so he asked the preacher and the congregation at his church to pray for him. Prayer was the church's ritual. Sam had faith in that. Chemotherapy was the doctor's. He had faith in that, too. In addition, at TLC we taught him what he could do for himself. He was willing to try with an open mind and allow that he could make a difference in his own healing process.

"I don't mind dying," he told us. "My productive life is over anyway. I just feel bad for the people I'd be leaving behind. For their sake, I'd like to stick around a little while longer. At least until I'm sure they'll be okay."

Together with Sam and his family, we created a multifaceted program specifically designed to serve him. For fifteen minutes three to five times a day, Sam imagined his immune cells, which he chose to picture as fighter jets, bombing and strafing hordes of little enemy aliens, which represented cancer cells. The defending jets were twelve times the size of the enemy aliens and outnumbered the bad guys ten to one. We also walked him through a daydream that guided him toward two significant life-style changes. He found out he had to pursue his dream of being a writer and have some fun every day. He and his wife started taking daily walks, collecting and polishing rocks, visiting beautiful state parks, going on picnics, listening to comedy tapes and records, renting movies for their VCR, and playing games. His wife reminded him that he loved to make up stories and made him promise to write them down. Reluctantly, he agreed to do all these things and kept it up for the first few months.

After three months, Sam was off all pain medication,

gaining weight, and feeling fit as a fiddle. He even beat an eighteen-year-old at tennis. During a regular checkup, he learned that the blood test for cancer activity showed a 70 percent improvement, his liver was functioning perfectly, and the tumor was shrinking. The doctor said he'd never seen this type of cancer go into remission and that Sam should consider himself lucky. He also told Sam he had no idea what had caused this stroke of luck. "Just keep doing whatever it is you've been doing," was his advice.

Sam, who had always had trouble with what he called "my self-concept," didn't follow his doctor's advice. When he realized that what he was doing was getting a new lease on life, he found himself wondering whether he was worthy of receiving such a miracle, and if he would know what to do with another twenty years of life. Slipping back into his old life-style, he slacked up on the visual imagery and instead of writing and having fun every day, went back to worrying and mourning over the death of his ego, the accountant. Three months later, right on schedule, in spite of continuing prayers and chemotherapy, Sam passed away peacefully.

Taking care of the bottom line, the accountant left his wife of forty years a new car, a new house, adequate funds, and a family of grown children who loved her and would take care of her. So he knew she'd be okay. His wife, who always worried that he couldn't make it on his own if she died first, took some small comfort in the fact that this, at least, worked out the way she hoped it would.

Why did Sam get better for a while only to turn around and die? All we can do is guess. Maybe, a combination of visual imagery, religious faith, and life-style change activated his immune system and directed it to attack the tumor. One part of him, the part that wanted to live, did that. Then, the part of him that would just as soon be dead took over and called the whole thing off.

One person, two minds. Maybe even three.

9

The We in Us

I am a double-minded man.
WILLIAM SHAKESPEARE

A car pulls up to the drive-in window of a bank. The driver, Bert, wants to cash a check. The teller asks if he can identify himself. Bert points the rearview mirror at his face, looks into it, and says, "Yep, that's me all right."

He knew the face because he saw it before—that very morning, in the bathroom mirror, staring out at him. It looked older than he knew he was. "Wow!" he thought while watching it shaving. "Is that me?" Logically, it couldn't be. It was in there, behind the glass. He was out here, in front of it. And everyone knows, one person can't be in two places at one time. In spite of that and in spite of himself, the part of Bert that believed personal appearance—how we look—is who we are, identified with it. Another part in each of us knows there's more to being a human—a person like you—than meets the eye.

Do you ever argue with yourself? Almost everyone does. That's why so many alarm clocks have a ten-minute nap setting. Bert used his to settle an argument the morning he had to get up early to cash the check. When the buzzer yanked him out of a pleasant dream into a workaday Monday morning, a big part of him, the part that always knows what he feels like doing, wanted to squelch it and go back to sleep. Another part, the responsible part that only knows what he should be doing, wouldn't hear of it. That's when the argument started—a silent argument inside his head.

"I can't face it. It's not fair. The world won't end if I sleep in just this once."

"If I don't cash that check first thing this morning, I'll have problems all day. I knew I shouldn't have stayed up to watch that stupid movie last night. Mr. Irresponsible—that's me. This is no way to be. I've just got to drag myself out of this bed and get going right now."

"Ten minutes. Maybe I can take just ten more minutes. That won't hurt anything."

"Okay, ten minutes. After that, right into the shower. No more stalling."

Bert pushed the nap button on the alarm clock. The buzzing stopped. Now, for ten minutes, he could relax. Both sides satisfied, argument settled. Which raises an interesting question: If there was only one person in the room, who was arguing with whom?

Back in 1981, Dr. Roger Sperry won a Nobel prize in medicine for answering that question and for redefining the word "I." His split-brain studies suggest that each of us has at least two distinct minds, and they sometimes argue with one another. Sperry's typical split-brain patient is a person in whom lines of communication between left and right brains have been cut to treat intractable epilepsy, tumors, or other medical conditions.

116

After recovery, a number of patients agreed to let Dr. Sperry test them to see how the operation had affected their minds. In our description of these tests, we will, for the sake of simplicity and clarity, take some liberties with details. Essentially, here's what happened.

Picture a bowl of fruit sitting on a table. There's an apple, an orange, a peach, and a pear. Seated at the same table, with a patch over her right eye, is a split-brain patient. Let's call her Carol. Carol knows what's in the bowl, but it's covered with a cloth so she can't see the fruit. Behind the bowl is a TV screen.

To follow what happens next, you need to know that each brain runs the opposite side of the body and looks out at the world through the opposite eye. With her right eye covered, Carol's left brain is completely in the dark and can't see what's going on. The words "Please pick up the orange" appear on the screen. Nothing happens. Using only her left eye, Carol can see the words but has no idea what they mean. Obviously, the right brain can't read. Now, a picture of a hand picking up an orange appears on the screen. This time, Carol gets the message. She sends her left hand under the cloth and into the bowl, where it gropes around and fishes out the orange. Apparently, the right brain *can* read. Not words, but pictures.

Now the doctor moves the patch to cover the other eye to see what the left brain can and cannot do on its own. The image of a hand picking up a pear appears on the screen. Nothing happens. Using only her right eye, Carol has no idea what she's looking at or what she's supposed to do. Her left brain can't read the image. The image fades and is replaced by a sentence— "Please pick up the pear." Words the right eye can see, the left brain can read, comprehend, and respond to. It sends Carol's right hand under the napkin and into the bowl. It gropes around, but it can't tell one fruit from another, so it would seem that the left brain can't read shapes.

Now, the patch comes off so Carol can watch what's happening with both eyes. Pointing to the orange she still holds in her left hand, the doctor asks if she can tell him what it is. She can't. The name is on the tip of her tongue, but she can't quite recall it. Her right brain recognizes the shape but knows nothing about names. Her left brain could name it if it could recognize the shape, but it can't because that information is on the other side. With lines of communication cut, it's impossible to combine one way of knowing with the other—the way you're doing right now.

Your left brain reads the words on this page and transmits their meaning, like telephone messages, to the other side, where your right brain converts them to images of a lady with an eye patch sitting at a table, watching a TV screen, and touching fruit.

Now comes the most fascinating part of the experiment. Still pointing to the orange, the doctor asks her where she got it. Carol hasn't a clue. Her right brain, which got her to pick it up, knows where, but it doesn't speak or understand words so it can't answer the question. Her left brain, which understands what the doctor wants to know, had its eye covered when Carol retrieved the orange, so it never saw that happen and can't answer the question either.

We seem to be dealing with two distinct brains. Each with a mind of its own. When Carol fished the orange out of the bowl, one of her minds was absent. It couldn't see, so it didn't know what the other was doing.

You don't have to split your brains or close an eye to become absentminded. It happens to normal people all the time—even to you. Have you ever gotten so involved in conversation, reading, or TV that you didn't realize how many potato chips, peanuts, or chocolates, you had eaten until you noticed the empty space where they used to be? Even with the wiring intact, left and right brains can disconnect and operate independently—the way they do when you meet someone whose face is familiar, but the name escapes you. Or run across the name of a person you know you know, but you can't remember the face. In the first case, your right brain remembered, but your left brain forgot. In the second, it's the other way around.

Down below and in between these two is a third brain—the hindbrain. A lot older and much younger than the ones Dr. Sperry worked with, the hindbrain also has a mind of its own. Time-wise, it's the oldest. It developed first and grew the other two the way a calf grows horns. Functionally, it's the youngest, because its mind is the mind of a child. It's the one who wants to sleep in on Monday mornings and who eats chocolates while the others aren't watching.

119

With Dr. Sperry's help, we've disassembled the biocomputer brain and examined its component parts. Wired together and working inside our skulls, they operate as a unit that constitutes the three-in-one being we all call "I." Now that we've put it back together again, let's have a look at how it works.

Psychologically, each of us is a triple personality—a nuclear family. Alive and well in every man is an inner woman. Sex change operations prove that. A snip here, a tuck there, a few hormone shots, and there she is in the flesh. For grown men and women, the feminine personality is the mind of the right brain. She lives in a world of images and communicates through facial expressions and body language. Messages from Gaia come through her as dreams and visions. She also uses visual images to program personal experiences. The anthropologist Julian Jaynes estimates that she is at least thirty-five thousand years old. Nurturing life and creating beauty and loving relationships are what make her feel good.

In both sexes, the analytical, goal-oriented masculine personality lives in the left brain in a world of words. Dr. Jaynes estimates him to be at least eight thousand years old. Before that time, he says, we humans didn't know about words, so this aspect of us couldn't function. Without words, he couldn't construct belief systems, explain how things really are, or decide how they should be. Words are the tools he uses to make thoughts, which program personal reality and carry messages from Gaia. Messages from Gaia come through him as inspirational thoughts and fresh ideas. In the game of life, he plays to win—which means always being right and in control.

Psychologists call this aspect of awareness the Ego or the Intellect. We've been calling him the Thinker. Some three hundred years ago, a philosopher named Descartes won a permanent place in history books when he said, "I think, therefore I am." People who buy into his belief tend to identify with the thinker and to ignore their other two personalities. As a result, they forget two-thirds of who they really are.

Once upon a time, before time was, there was a Greek named Narcissus. He lived out in space just beyond the edge of time and acted like some kind of god. One day, he dropped down to the lake for a drink. In the water, he saw a beautiful face. He smiled, and his new friend smiled back. That did it. Narcissus was head over heels in love. In a fit of passion, he jumped on the object of his affection, fell into the lake, and drowned.

This story is a metaphor for what happens when people become so taken with their image that they lose themselves in it. You don't need to fall into a lake for this to happen. Your reflected image in the mirror can swallow you up just as completely. Whether you fall in love with it or decide you hate it, the result is the same. This is because love and hate are two sides of a single coin—the opposite of which is indifference. When you know that what you're looking at is not the real you, you're less likely to submerge yourself in it. So who's looking?

There is a part of you, an inner child, that feels exactly the way you did when you were two. It still answers to your name and looks out through your eyes in utter amazement as it watches your body grow older and change. It lives in your hindbrain and relates to neither your name nor your physical appearance. This is because it has the intelligence of an amoeba. But don't let that fool you. The oldest and wisest of the three, the mind in your hindbrain is in a sense as old as life itself—some four billion years old. On its own, it has all the know-how necessary to keep your body alive and well without your having to think about it.

An amoeba is a single-celled, brainless creature. It doesn't even have a head to put a brain in. When you look at one through a microscope, all you see is a tiny little blob that moves by oozing. Put it in between a drop of acid and a drop of nourishment and, ten times out of ten, it will retreat from the poison and move toward the food. Which proves that, on some level, it can tell the difference between pleasure and pain. It can also find food, devour and digest it, eliminate what it doesn't need, and reproduce. When simpleminded or even brainless creatures exhibit complex, purposeful behavior without knowing how or why they're doing what they're doing, we say they're acting out of instinct. If that's so, instincts must have been around a lot longer than brains.

Without knowing how or why, when you were newborn, you cried when hungry, suckled when fed, slept when satisfied, and relieved yourself when you felt the urge. Seventy-five trillion tiny single cells acting as one. All orchestrated by the circuitry in your hindbrain, the mechanism that transmits the intelligence that guided your body's evolution from fertilized egg to fully formed fetus and through the three stages of birth without your having to give it a single thought. This intelligence can guide you for as long as you live.

We're talking about the intelligence that makes plants grow and turn their leaves toward the light. The know-how that keeps your heart beating whether or not you pay it any mind. We believe it exists independently of brains or any other physical structure—that brains, like radio receivers, tune into it. The left brain converts it into thoughts; the right into pictures; and our inner child, the mind in the hindbrain, turns it into feelings—inner urges and sensations of pleasure and pain.

Three minds, each with a brain of its own, living in one body. Sometimes, they fight. When they do, the body becomes a battleground. If you ask the right questions, they will tell you what the fight is about and what you need to do to settle it.

When Mary Sue's grandpa died and left her a pile of money, she bought herself an elegant motor home equipped with a state-of-the-art word processor. Her plan was to spend a year touring the country and writing a book—something she had always wanted to do but never could find the time for, not to mention the funds. Her children were grown and her ex-husband had remarried, so this was a perfect opportunity for her creative personality, the writer in her, to come out and blossom. Her inner child loved the idea because it sounded like fun. The thinker in her left brain wasn't so sure. . . . she thought she'd be better off putting the money into a sound investment. After we worked with her a while, she reluctantly agreed to go along with the scheme on the off chance that she might be able to sell the book. She'd been on the road for about three months when she called us from a state park in Utah.

"I've got this incredible stiff neck. It hurts like hell. Kept me up all night. I'm way out here in the boondocks, so I can't even get to a drugstore to get aspirin. It feels as if this hand has me by the scruff of the neck and is squeezing real hard. It seems to be a woman's hand. When I picture it letting go, the pain eases, but as soon as I try to do something else, relax, or get some sleep, it clamps down again. Do you have any suggestions about what I might do next to help me deal with this thing?"

Now that we knew what ailed her, we followed up with a variation on Parsifal's second question: "What is it the stiff neck keeps you from doing that you would be doing if you didn't have it?"

Mary Sue thought for a moment then said, "Driving, I guess. Under the circumstances, that's out of the question. I can't turn my head in either direction to check traffic, and even if I put my hands on the steering wheel and try to turn that, I get a shot of pain."

"Suppose you were stuck right where you are for the next week," we asked. "What would you do then?"

"Write, I suppose," she said. "To tell you the truth,

I haven't written a word since I started out three months ago. Every time I sit down at the computer to write something, a part of me—I guess it's my rational mind—judges it before I even get it down. He says he doesn't think I have any talent so what's the sense of even trying."

"In your mind's eye, can you see the woman's hand that's got you by the scruff of your neck right now?"

"Sure."

"Can you mentally zoom back, like a TV camera, and see the woman whose hand it is?"

Mary Sue told us that she could see the woman and that she looked really angry. We suggested that, on her next out breath, she imagine herself asking the woman what she was mad about, and then to empty her mind and watch what thoughts came into it while she was breathing in. Mary Sue did that and started to laugh.

"She says if that bastard won't let her write, she won't let him drive. I guess she's talking about the critical part of me I call the judge. I tell you, he's a real pain in the neck."

That image really tickled her funny bone. At our suggestion, she imagined the judge and the writer negotiating. She said she'd unhand the scruff of his neck if he'd promise to back off and let her write without bugging her for two to four hours a day starting right now. The judge said, "Okay," they shook hands, and almost immediately the pain eased, her neck muscles relaxed, and Mary Sue could move her head.

"That's amazing," she said.

"What's amazing to us," we said, "is that more people don't know about this."

They say an ounce of prevention is worth a pound of cure. The best time to handle this kind of conflict is before it starts. To do this, you have to balance the needs and desires of your three personalities on a day-to-day basis.

We all know how wonderful it feels to be alive on some days. What do we do differently on those days that makes them so enjoyable? Maybe it's just luck or the law of averages, you say. This may be part of it. But our attitude toward and our awareness of what's going on within us and all around us also have a role to play in setting the tone for any given day.

We can all improve the quality of our lives—one day at a time. An easy way to begin is to plan to put some *balance* into each day. In the morning, on a sheet of paper, write these three headings: TODAY'S RESPON-SIBILITIES, TODAY'S SIMPLE PLEASURES, TODAY'S CHILDLIKE FUN. Under each heading, write the first three activities that come to mind.

Under RESPONSIBILITIES, you might list things such as: pay bills, read documents, grocery shop. Under SIM-PLE PLEASURES: hot bath, leisurely walk, tend plants. Under CHILDLIKE FUN: fly a kite, hot fudge sundae, funny movie. As you go through the day, accomplish at least two of the three activities in each category.

The next morning, start with a blank page and allow yourself to begin a brand new day. Don't, for example, turn yesterday's fun into a chore by putting it on today's list even though you don't really feel like doing it again. You can list brief activities (make a phone call, read a poem, listen to a favorite tune, sing in the shower) on days you expect to be very busy. Then, on days when you have more time, take affirmative action to correct the balance. Make sure to spend extra time relaxing with simple pleasures and childlike fun.

This balancing act gets easier with practice, and we've found the rewards are numerous: peace of mind, joy, the satisfaction of accomplishment, and a heightened sense of well-being. As you continue to use this technique, you will notice yourself experiencing more and more "good days." String enough of these together, and you've got yourself a good life.

10

The Magic Theater

Imagination is more important than knowledge.
ALBERT EINSTEIN

Brenda and Bert found a beautiful driftwood specimen on the beach and decided to haul it home. One end was thick and gnarled with a flat surface on which it could stand upight. From there, it tapered down to a thin cylinder with a beautiful filigree pattern. One on each side, they picked it up by the thick end and started dragging it toward the parking lot. It was very heavy, and the going was slow. Just as it began to look as if they weren't going to make it, a man, who had been watching them, suggested they try hauling it by the skinny end. That way, he said, the bulk of the weight would rest on the sand and just slide along behind them.

"Isn't it amazing," Bert said as they followed the man's suggestion, "how much easier life is when you do things right?"

"It sure is, dearie," Brenda said, "except that we're getting farther away from the car."

This story illustrates what the philosopher Nietzsche was talking about when he said that the dumbest thing we humans do is forget what we started out to do. Some people spend their lives chasing wealth, status, and material possessions when what they really want is contentment and peace of mind. If what they're doing gets far enough out of alignment with their true purpose, they're likely to experience some adversity that wakes them up and gets them back on track.

We know a woman who had been swallowing tranquilizer pills, three a day, for ten years. She was in real estate, on a tight time schedule, and, as she put it, "a nervous wreck." She started taking the pills hoping they would calm her down. They didn't. She kept taking them anyway because she was afraid that if she stopped, she'd get even worse. It was hard to see how that could be possible. The goal-directed male in her left brain was hooked on the belief that peace and contentment come only with financial security. So she started a real estate company to make enough money to be secure and feel content. Money was the means by which she hoped to achieve that end. Before she realized what was happening, the means became the end. Her ego, the real estate mogul, got her so involved in building an empire and making money that she forgot why she had started doing this in the first place.

One day, she came down with pneumonia. After a week in bed, even though she still felt totally exhausted, she decided she was well enough to get actively involved in closing a very lucrative deal. Her doctor wasn't so sure, but, business-wise, it was the right thing to do so she did. And she did it right. On the way home, she had a dizzy spell, fell, and broke her right arm—the one she signs checks and other important business documents with.

The Magic Theater

If you stub your toe, lock the keys in the car, or misplace a credit card, you can't blame anyone else. You have to admit you did it yourself—absentmindedly or on purpose. One of your minds did it while the others weren't watching. To find out why, you need to communicate with the culprit. Actually, the incident itself is a signal from a part of you that's being neglected. To get the message you have to ask yourself, "Why me?"

When we use the word "I," we're talking about purpose, not cause. Identifying the cause for her pneumonia didn't help the woman with the broken arm one bit. Since the pneumonia was a drug-resistant virus, it didn't even help her doctor treat it. Knowing that the fall was caused by a drop in blood pressure that happened because she went back to work too soon didn't help her feel any better either. It just made her feel frustrated. When we suggested that her troubles might be serving a purpose, she got even more frustrated.

"Are you suggesting that I gave myself pneumonia and broke my own arm on purpose? Why would anyone in their right mind do a thing like that?" That night, she had a dream. "I was in the cabin of an express train that was headed in the wrong direction and picking up speed. No matter what I said or did, the guy driving it wouldn't stop or even slow down. So I started hollering for help. Up ahead, a little kid was sitting beside the tracks. He heard me holler and tossed a yellow gum ball onto the track, which derailed the train and woke me up."

Dreams are a communication channel through which our unconscious minds reveal the purpose of what's

131

happening in our lives. The problem is, they're hard to remember and even harder to decipher. So we read books or consult experts to tell us what they mean. More often than not, the interpretation is as obscure as the dream itself.

If you'd like to try your hand at interpreting your own dreams, here's a rule of thumb that might make it easier. Assume that every character in the dream is an aspect of yourself. In the case of the woman who broke her arm, the man driving the train in the wrong direction was her inner male—the real estate mogul in her left brain. The woman who wanted to slow things down and turn them around, and found herself trapped in the same vehicle with a crazy man, was her feminine personality. The kid that saved the day with a golden gum ball was her inner child. This interpretation, which was her own, helped her understand the purpose of the accident and reorder her priorities.

If you're lucky, a figure might appear in a dream and explain in clear, simple language the meaning of what's going on in your life and what you need to do about it. For thousands of years, humans have been going on vision quests and consulting shamans to help them get in touch with these inner guides. Throughout the ages, people have ingested hallucinogenic (vision-generating) herbs such as peyote and mescaline to expedite the process. Even today, members of so-called primitive cultures and a fair number of sophisticated moderns still do. Author Jane Roberts conjured up a wise old adviser without any outside help and wrote several books about what he (Seth) had to say about reality and life in general.

Severe stress can also trigger the appearance of an imaginary teacher who tells you exactly what you have to do to get through this particular crisis. During a radio interview, a former nurse described how it happened for her.

"I had two miscarriages back to back, which weakened my body tremendously. During one of those miscarriages, I hemorrhaged. Suddenly, I realized that I was out of my body. I was above the bed looking down at it. I didn't want to go back in that body. And, for a moment in time, I was in an expanded state of consciousness where I really had a choice. Then, I had what I guess psychiatrists would call a hallucination. For me, it was real. It was a visitation from a being that I thought at the time was Jesus. He told me to stay in my body for a while. He told me that I had a mission—something to do in the world—the awakening of the divine child within that I feel must awaken for each of us in every lifetime. The next thing I knew, I was back in my hospital bed fighting for my own life again."

The woman who told this story said the experience changed her life. As a result of it, she founded an institute dedicated to helping people get in touch with and liberate the part of themselves she calls "the divine child within."

You don't have to struggle to remember your dreams, swallow mind-altering drugs, go out of your body, or have a close encounter with death to conjure up an all-

133

knowing inner adviser. Daydreaming can make it happen with much less hassle. Daydreams tap the same creative source night dreams do. Since they happen while you're wide awake, understanding or remembering what they're trying to teach you is no problem. What's more, in a daydream, you get to pick your own inner expert. With the technique we teach at TLC, you get to choose three — one from each mind. The technique is simple, easy, and fun — as easy as picturing a cartoon character.

Try it. Picture a cartoon character — one you've seen on the TV, at the movies, in the funny papers, or in a book. What you're looking at is a memory picture, a hologram generated by the circuitry of your biocomputer brain. Imagine yourself waving at it. Notice that it waves back. That's because the biocomputer is interactive. Keep your mind's eye on the image and watch what happens. Watching animates it. It will start moving and doing silly stuff that will probably make you laugh.

Recall what physics professor Cindy said back in Chapter 3 about the white rabbit and her magic castle being just as real as the teacher in the brick schoolhouse. Likewise, the images you conjure up with your imagination are every bit as real as the one you see in the mirror or the people you meet on the street. If you talk nicely to them and pay attention to what they have to say, they answer questions, give advice, and solve problems. That's why we call them "allies."

To start a conversation, divide your thoughts into two groups. Thoughts that go through your mind during expiration, while you're breathing out, are *your* thoughts.

While emptying your lungs, empty your mind. Then, as you slowly refill them, watch the thoughts, *inspirational* thoughts, that come in with your breath. Make believe they come from your allies. Connected to the breath, random thoughts turn into meaningful conversations. You'll probably feel as if you're talking to yourself. That's because you are. One of your minds is conversing with the others.

To start a conversation, think of a question that is weighing on your mind today—a matter you'd really like advice about. State it in terms a five-year-old child would understand. Keep it simple. On an out breath, imagine yourself putting that question to your imaginary friend. With the next in breath, expect an answer to pop into your mind. The answer you get will be so simple and so clear you'll wonder why you didn't think of it before. This is because you're now accessing brain circuits you don't ordinarily tap into.

Vince had trouble asking women out because he could never decide where to take them. Each date was a fiasco because he spent it worrying about whether his companion was having a terrible time because he took her to the wrong place. Now, he had a date with a woman he really liked, and he found himself in the same bind— only worse. This one, he really wanted to impress. As the big day approached, he was paralyzed by indecision and getting more and more stressed out. Asking an imaginary cartoon character for advice seemed silly to Vince, but it was preferable to calling off the date or running the risk of living through another disaster. So he pictured

Bugs Bunny. He said the rabbit was leaning against a tree, chewing on a carrot. He imagined himself waving at it, but the image of Bugs just stood there, staring at him. Vince wondered why Bugs didn't wave back.

"Ask him," we suggested.

Vince imagined himself doing this during his next out breath and started to laugh. "He says, why should he, I'm not even real."

"Tell him," we said, "you're at least as real as he is."

Vince did this, and the rabbit chuckled and offered him a bite of his carrot. Then, Vince imagined himself asking, "How do you make friends with a female?"

"Easy," said Bugs. "I just tell her I'm going out to play and have some fun and invite her to come along."

For Vince, this was a revelation. It never occurred to him that he could plan a good time for himself and invite a lady friend to come along and join him. He tried it, and it worked.

Clara had no problem relating to members of the opposite sex, but she was afraid of the dark. When her husband was home, it was okay. When he was away, she slept with the lights on. Once, while he was on a business trip, there was a power outage. The flashlight was out, too—dead batteries. So there she was, alone in the dark in the middle of the night. Screams of panic were out of the question because she didn't want to wake the neighbors or involve the police. For a while, it was touch and go but in the end, embarrassment kept the lid on terror long enough for her to deal with it.

"I took five slow, deep breaths and pictured myself

in a peaceful meadow on a bright, sunny day. Then, with my mind's eye, I looked around for a living creature. On a tree stump, about three feet from where I was sitting I saw a friendly looking owl. It seemed to me his name was Howland. Sitting at the base of the stump, looking up at Howland, was a baby chipmunk I decided to call Squeaky. As long as I kept my eyes closed, my breathing regular, and my mind on that image, I could remain calm. I must have dozed off because next thing I knew, it was daylight. I guess you could say I converted a nightmare into a pleasant dream."

Like many of the fears lots of people have, fear of the dark is childish and irrational. So mature, reasoned arguments don't make a dent in it. To dissolve an irrational fear, we need to apply a basic law of chemistry (like dissolves like) and find an irrational solution. As it did for Vince, pure fantasy, a daydream, worked for Clara.

To change an attitude, you have to start by separating yourself from it. So we asked Clara to picture herself back in the meadow with Howland and Squeaky and to make believe one of them was afraid of the dark. She said she guessed that would be the chipmunk. In her daydream, the problem was his, not hers. That way, she put some distance between herself and it. Then, we asked her to dream up a fantasy with a happy ending in which the problem gets solved. "Make it up as you go along," we told her. "Keep your mind's eye on your allies, think about a happy ending, and see what comes to you."

Clara decided Squeaky had come to Howland for advice. The wise old owl asked him what was so scary about plain old dark. "The bogeyman man," said Squeaky. "I'm scared the bogeyman man will come out of it and eat me all up."

Howland opened an enormous book, read a few pages, and said, "It says here the bogeyman man never eats chipmunks. He tried one a thousand years ago and it tasted awful. It made him sick for a week. He's quoted as saying he wouldn't eat chipmunk if you served him one on a silver platter." Squeaky giggled and ran off, happy as a clam. Then, Howland opened another book entitled *Clara's Destiny*. He read some, looked at Clara, and said, "It says here you are definitely not destined to be gobbled up by a bogeyman man in this lifetime. You can run along now if you like and play with Squeaky. You're both perfectly safe." Clara isn't afraid of the dark anymore. The cure was as nonsensical as the cause. She remembered that when she was very young, her brothers used to tease her with stories about a bogeyman man who skulked around in the dark looking for little girls to gobble up. Howland's reassurance was a perfect antidote to those stories. She still burns the night-light when her husband is away out of force of habit. But she doesn't lose any sleep worrying about power outages.

The images projected by our biocomputer brains (one masculine, one feminine, one childlike) come in an infinite variety of forms. You don't know what you're going to get until you look. A businessman who needed advice on how to raise cash visualized a word processor as his male ally. He just closed his eyes, looked around, and there it was, ready to serve. Answers to his questions and advice came to him as printout on an imaginary video display terminal. Halfway through the session, he said he had to leave. "My inner guide just gave me a fantastic idea, and I have to get to a phone right away to implement it."

The most impressive ally we ever came across was conjured up by a sophisticated-looking lady in New York City. It happened during a seminar we were doing for women executives. The participants were sitting with their eyes closed, imagining themselves in a beautiful place, and looking around for a male ally. Suddenly, the lady in question let out a gasp, opened her eyes wide, and stood up. She was physically shaken.

"I saw God!" she said. "I picked heaven as the most beautiful place I could think of, looked around with my mind's eye, and there he was, gray beard and all. Looking at me."

"So what's wrong with that?" we asked. "Lots of people picture God and imagine themselves talking to him when they need advice."

"But I'm an atheist!" she said, still trembling.

When we explained that what she was looking at wasn't actually God himself, but only a hologram printed out by the circuitry of her right brain, she heaved a huge sigh of relief, said, "Thank God!," sat down, and said she was ready to go on with the process.

The images we see in these daydreams, like those that come to us in night dreams, are all aspects of ourselves.

The lady in New York was comfortable with the idea that the image of God she saw represented the aspect of herself that creates and sets the rules for her personal world. Her female ally was Aphrodite, Greek goddess of love, and the little kid in her was represented by Puck, a magical child from a Shakespearean play. Does this give you some idea about what kind of person she is?

Even though they are figments of our own creative imagination, our allies, once we start paying attention to them, seem to take on lives of their own. We can never know in advance what they might do or say next. Authors, playwrights, or scriptwriters will tell you the same about the characters they invent. Empty I AM-NESS is the inventor. All the author has to do is be quiet and watch the show.

Watching our allies interact gives us a chance to step outside ourselves and observe the play of our own consciousness. This process creates powerful insights into why we act the way we do. Have you ever struggled with a problem for hours or even days and gotten nowhere? Then, when you least expect it, a light bulb seems to go on in your head and illuminate the solution. That's the kind of insight we're talking about.

Dorothy was on her way downtown to meet a social obligation. A sorority sister she hadn't seen for twenty years had called yesterday to say she was in town and could they "do lunch" at her hotel. Starting out to the car for the two-hour drive, Dorothy fished in her purse for the keys. They were gone. There was a spare set in the glove compartment, but the car doors were locked, which was odd because she never locked the car after she put it in the garage. She must have done it absent-mindedly last night. One of her minds did it while the others weren't watching. But which one? And why?

Whenever you find yourself in this kind of frustrating situation, instead of gnashing your teeth, yelling, and swearing (or after you've gotten all that out of your system), you might think about Parsifal's second question: What purpose does this serve? Dorothy spent an hour storming around the house, hunting for her lost keys. Finally, she ran out of gas and just stood there, staring at the wall and watching her thoughts. Her first thought was about purpose. What was losing her keys making her do that she wouldn't do if this hadn't happened? The answer came in a flash: canceling the luncheon appointment with her sorority sister, Daphne. "But I want to have lunch with Daphne," she said out loud. "So why did I lose my keys and lock the spare set in the car?" she wondered. The word *dimwit* crossed her mind. Then it occurred to her that as badly as part of her wanted to meet this social obligation, another wanted out of it. Finally, she decided that instead of spending the day spinning her wheels and beating up on herself, she'd do better to settle the argument and get her head together through a daydream.

As soon as she pictured her allies (Mama Bear, Papa Bear, and Baby Bear), Dorothy got her first clue about what was going on. Mama Bear was pacing the floor and growling. The other two were sitting in their chairs smiling. Correlating this scene with the day's events, she realized that part of her, her feminine personality, was upset and frustrated about having to break the appointment. She imagined Mama Bear putting it this way, "When a sorority sister calls to invite us for lunch, we go no matter what it takes. You don't sabotage me by playing stupid games with keys and car doors!" She seemed to be talking to the other two, who weren't smiling anymore. Obviously, they and Mama Bear didn't see eye to eye on this matter.

Carrying the process a step further, Dorothy imagined herself asking who locked the spare keys in the car last night. Papa Bear raised his paw. He said there were some important things he had planned to get done today and driving into town and back was not one of them. Mama Bear apologized for not consulting him before agreeing to do this. Dorothy realized she had accepted the invitation on the spur of the moment, without giving her own plans a single thought. She must have been upset about that when she absentmindedly locked herself out of her car. Papa Bear did it while Mama Bear wasn't watching. He derailed her plans for the day to show her how it felt when she torpedoed his. Mama and Papa forgave each other and exchanged bear hugs. Watching them do this made Dorothy feel much better. Frustration and anger drained from her body, leaving her calm and relaxed.

Then, she asked who "disappeared" the keys out of her purse. Baby Bear hid under the bed. She imagined herself coaxing it out, setting it in her lap, and gently asking why. The cub's response was visual rather than verbal. It disappeared out of her lap and reappeared on the table, dressed in a forest ranger's hat, ranger pants, and a wide belt—a miniature version of Smokey the Bear with a little fire fighter's shovel in its left paw. With its right paw, it pointed to a smoking cigarette.

Dorothy felt a tickle in her throat, coughed, and got the message. She remembered that back in college, Daphne had been a chain-smoker. She probably still was. Even if she wasn't, having lunch in a hotel dining room meant sitting around for an hour or more in a room full of other people's cigarette smoke. The very thought of it made her cough again. When she accepted Daphne's invitation, she didn't give her distaste for cigarette smoke any more thought than she gave her plans for the day. Mama Bear looked embarrassed. She picked up Baby Bear, gave it a hug, and said she was sorry but still feeling pretty bad about having to break the date with her sorority sister.

When the three aspects of ourselves have a falling out and pull in opposite directions, nothing goes right. To turn things around, we have to negotiate a win-win-win consensus. Mama Bear would win if she could have lunch with Daphne, but it didn't have to be today. Papa Bear said if he could have the day to get his chores done, going tomorrow would be fine with him. The littlest bear was still unhappy about having to sit in a smoky room with a bunch of grown-ups. "Maybe we could go to the zoo," it said. "We could take a picnic, and you guys could talk while I feed the animals. That way, I could have some fun, too. As long as you tell Daphne not to blow smoke in my face."

143

Everyone liked that plan. Dorothy called Daphne, and she said that was fine with her. Then Dorothy called the locksmith, who said he could come out and unlock her car first thing in the morning. When he told her what it was going to cost, Papa Bear got really unhappy. Instead of fretting about that, Dorothy decided she might as well get on with her chores and start by doing a load of laundry. In the pocket of the slacks she had been wearing last night, she found her keys. In a beautifully coordinated operation, her inner child stuck them in there after Papa Bear had locked the car door.

Practical daydreaming, the process we're describing here, does much more than help people cope with life's little crises. It provides aid and comfort for those going through a radical life change. When a person's whole life seems to be falling apart, it's helpful to be able to recognize a pattern and see how what seems to be a catastrophe is actually preparation for the next stage of life.

She never thought it could happen to her. Louise was forty-two, smart, well traveled, and attractive. But, over the past two years, one problem after another had piled up until she was forced to find a way to deal with the whole mess. She was going through menopause with its aches and pains, heart palpitations, hot flashes, and depression. She had injured her right ankle and her left knee. Her mother was slowly dying two thousand miles away. And, to top it all off, her usually resourceful financial abilities were failing her. Scared, hobbling, and a bit numb with grief, she told us she had to find some solutions.

During her personal program at TLC, she began to see that, one day at a time, she could handle everything. She learned to do little things each day toward getting back on her feet, literally and figuratively. Her instructions came from within.

As she listened to her inner life-guidance system, Louise realized that some of her problems were the result of acute pleasure deficiency. She wasn't letting her inner child, one-third of herself, have any time. Little Orphan Annie (red curly hair and all) told Louise she did in her knee because she, Annie, was tired of being ignored. When Louise asked Annie what she'd like to do while they were here at the coast, Annie knew right away. "Let's go to the beach and fly a kite!"

Louise's male friend, a Jimmy Stewart look-alike named EZ, short for Ezekiel, was skeptical about doing this because it seemed like walking on the sand would be too much for the weak knee. A real catch-22 situation. Louise's third ally, Maid Marion from the story of Robin Hood, suggested that Louise just take it slow and stop if she felt any discontent.

As it turned out, Louise walked on the sand with no problem and got the kite up after her husband and children tried but failed. At her next session with us, she reported success. Her knee had improved 50 percent compared to before the kite flying. And she could now walk farther than she had in a couple of years. Since her program, Louise has called us to report that whenever the going gets tough, Louise goes kite flying. It works every time. FUN HEALS.

Louise also learned to put her problems in perspective. While talking with her allies in the mountain meadow she had chosen as her favorite place, she asked, "What can I do about all these awful things happening to me?"

As she looked at all three allies, Maid Marion answered, "You have to balance them." Louise wasn't sure what that meant, so she asked Marion to make it clearer. After a couple of deep breaths, Louise said Marion meant, "Pay attention to what's going well, too."

We told Louise about a game we play every day. All it takes is a sheet of paper. On the top we write:

What's right?　　**What's done?**　　**What made me feel good?**

Then, all through the day, we make entries in the three columns. This list gets us to notice life's simple pleasures and little miracles that otherwise slip by unmentioned or unnoticed. Another by-product of this is that we are careful to balance doing with watching and responsibilities with fun.

Louise began making daily lists. Until now, she had always had lists around of what must get done and when she planned to do it. She found that after making a habit of listing the day's positive side, her other lists became much less important to her. Yet, everything always got done on time anyway.

With this new view of her life, Louise began to see her knee and ankle trouble differently. It had a purpose—to slow her down and make her sit back with her feet up several times a day. This let her body rest and do the extra work required for her change of life while her allies fed her answers to whatever she asked. Gratitude began to replace frustration. Now, whenever she's resting, she first lists the day's good news and then spends a little time writing fairy tales and animal stories for her own child within. Her kids love the stories, too, so her relationship with them is becoming closer and more fun. She is even sending a few of her kids' favorite stories to publishers.

Lastly, Louise now sees the balance between her financial mess and her mother's death. Either without the other would have paralyzed her. Somehow, the fact that she was losing her mom made the money problem seem minor; conversely, the money problem was so immediate that she had to act decisively and soon. So sitting around grieving all day long was out of the question. Again, she felt grateful. Maybe she was actually going through all this to push her to become a children's book writer. It had always been her dream.

A single musical note, on its own, doesn't mean much. Set a group of them side by side, and you have a tune. Isolated incidents don't mean much either. Focus on them, and you won't see the forest for the trees. If you look for connections between experiences, you'll notice that they interrelate to form a pattern. Then, you've got a road map to guide you through the changes — like the one that helped Louise see how her trio of traumas was actually guiding her into a new career.

It's not unusual for a series of events headed for a

happy ending to start on a sour note. Louise's story is one example. Getting a flat tire and missing an airplane that crashes would be another. For Connie, it was a broken glass. She raised it to offer a toast, lost her grip, and down it went. The occasion was a party celebrating her promotion to the rank of major in charge of rehabilitation at a large army hospial. Some weeks later, on her way to work, she had a spell of double vision and almost drove off the road. This time, there was no alcohol involved so she guessed something else must be going on. She was right: multiple sclerosis (M.S.). The insulating material protecting her nerves was disintegrating, allowing them to short-circuit. As communications from her brain faltered, her muscles got progressively weaker and harder to control.

We know a lot about M.S. One thing we don't know is what causes it. This explains why medical science has not been able to come up with a cure. The doctrine of specificity, the bedrock foundation upon which contemporary medical practice rests, holds that every disease has a specific cause that must be treated with a specific remedy in order to get a cure. So, no known cause, no cure.

Connie knew this when she called us after reading a copy of *The Healing Mind*. Having worked with patients, she was well aware of what this disease could do to people. Determined to do whatever it took to keep that from happening to her, she met the first prerequisite for healing: clear intention. She was also open-minded enough to allow that this affliction was serving some purpose in her life—that it was a feedback signal that would disappear once she got the message and made the appropriate life change. What she needed from us was a technique to help her see what that change needed to be.

Connie's journey on the road to recovery began with a dream. She dreamed she was standing on the edge of a cliff looking down into the open mouth of an enormous tube. Then, she heard a voice say, "Once you go down that tube, there's no turning back." Besides, it was pitch black in there, and that was scary, so she woke up. A few nights later, the dream recurred. This time, curiosity overcame fear, and she jumped in. During our first session, she described what happened next.

"I felt like Alice in Wonderland falling down the rabbit hole, except that I was sliding down the tube at terrific speed. I was terrified. Then, I heard that voice again, asking me what I was afraid of. I said I didn't know. Maybe that was it—the unknown. The voice said if it was unknown how could I know it was something to be afraid of. That made sense, so I decided to relax and enjoy the ride. Suddenly, I felt like a kid on a roller coaster. It was scary, exciting, and wonderful all at the same time. Next thing I knew, I was in a cavern filled with golden light. On a ledge, overhanging a pool of blue water, I saw a young woman and a little dog. The woman was crying. That's when I woke up. What do you suppose it means? Do you think it might have something to do with my M.S.?"

We told her that she could find answers to those questions within herself by making up a daydream that

149

picked up where the night dream left off. Connie closed her eyes and pictured herself back in the cavern with the woman and the little dog. She decided to call the woman Marie and the dog Marty. She asked them if they knew who was stripping the insulation off her nerves. The dog wagged its tail, and Marie answered for both. She said they were working together. "I do the big nerves and Marty does the little ones."

Connie asked Marie why they would do a thing like that, and Marie pointed toward the door. There, standing stiffly at attention, was an army officer with a stone face. "I'm not talking about his expression," Connie said, "I'm talking about his face. It's actually made of stone." Marie went on to say that she and Marty were stripping Connie's nerves to attract her attention and to send a signal to the guy guarding the door.

Connie still couldn't understand what it all meant. When we suggested that she see each character as an aspect of herself (again, a good rule for interpreting any dream), she got it. If the stone-faced officer guarding the door represented her ego, the major, then this fantasy was an accurate thumbnail sketch of her life in the army.

Her military career began the year women were first admitted to West Point. Back then, female officers were expected to out-macho their male counterparts to prove they had successfully subjugated their femaleness. If Marie represented Connie's femininity, and Marty her inner child, the image of the two of them on the shelf, under guard in an underground cavern, was a perfect portrayal of what she had been willing to do to advance her career.

"Two-thirds of me hasn't seen the light of day in years," she said. "I haven't been willing to have any fun or get romantically involved because it might damage my image. Would you believe I don't even own a pretty dress? Just perfectly pressed uniforms." There were tears in Connie's eyes. For the first time in who knows how long, Marie was out full blast. "I'm not that old, you know. Now, I'm looking at dying without ever having lived. Stupid, stupid, stupid!"

"A dying is required," we agreed. "But it doesn't have to be physical. On that point, negotiations are possible."

"How do I do that?" Connie asked.

"Imagine the major asking the other two what their price is for restoring the integrity of the circuitry. What do you suppose their terms might be?"

"That's easy," said Connie. "Take them off the shelf and let them out of the cavern. That would mean giving in to feelings and emotions and not constantly being guided by strict rules, rigid regulations, and career considerations. To do that, I'd have to quit the army. The major would never agree to that. I can hear him now, saying he'd rather die than surrender."

"That can be arranged," we said. "But he doesn't have to take everyone else, including Connie, with him. That is, unless you feel physical death is preferable to ego death. In either case, it looks like the major has had it. Kaput. Finished. What went down the tubes when you dropped that glass at the party was your military career.

Seems like Marie is letting you know you can either let it go or go down with it."

Suddenly, Connie was laughing. She said she could see Marty and Marie in full battle gear, preparing to execute a bayonet charge and, with it, the major. They looked comical, but she knew they were deadly serious. "Okay," she said. "I get the message. I'll put in for a medical discharge, retire the major, and go back to being a woman full-time." Then, Connie pictured herself and her allies on a tropical island. Marie was sitting under a coconut tree playing a guitar. Marty was cavorting on the beach and in the surf, having a wonderful time. Her male ally, who now looked like Robert Redford in casual dress, was still standing guard. Only now, he was protecting the other two rather than imprisoning them.

Three months later, we got a letter from Connie telling us she was out of the army, alive and well and living on Maui. "When we first got to Hawaii, we visited the Arizona Memorial and dropped a lei into the water in memory of the major. Now, I spend most of my time visiting friends, playing guitar, swimming and sunning myself on the beach. Double vision has not recurred, my muscular strength and coordination have significantly improved, and at this writing, I have no, repeat *no*, symptoms. Except for some calluses on my fingers from the guitar strings."

It has been a year since we first saw Connie. She still stays in touch by phone. She now has pretty clothes, a dog named Marty, and lots of friends, one of whom is more than just a friend. She's writing a book about her experiences and says her M.S. is still in remission. "I don't use the word *cured* because the military taught me always to keep my guard up when dealing with a dangerous adversary. As long as I keep the three parts of me balanced on a daily basis, I'm okay. If I can keep this up, one day at a time, for the next fifty or so years, I will have achieved my primary objective."

It was tough for a hard-nosed realist like the major to look to imaginary dream figures for guidance. This was a radical departure from standard operating procedure—medical as well as military. Connie was able to justify resorting to unorthodox tactics on the basis of what the military calls "expediency." According to this "end justifies the means" doctrine, it's okay to bend or even break regulations if doing this helps achieve an authorized objective.

In our experience, people with a spiritual orientation are able to accept inner guidance as a matter of faith. One time, we were invited to demonstrate our practical daydreaming technique for a group of ministers interested in exploring new ways of nurturing themselves. During the past year, five of their number had left the ministry because of burnout. The rest were looking for ways to keep it from happening to them. They were quite receptive to the notion that answers to the problems could be found within themselves by supplementing prayer and meditation with visual imagery. To show them how, we led them through a simple, four-step procedure:

1. Picture yourself in a beautiful place.
2. With your mind's eye, look around and you'll become aware of the presence of three living creatures. One male, one female, one child.
3. On your out breath, think of a question.
4. As you inhale, watch for an answer.

At the end of the exercise, when all eyes were open again, a bubbly reverend shared what happened for her.

"I know my new little friends are going to teach me a lot. I visualized myself in the high Sierra, in a meadow full of wildflowers. In my mind's eye, three nature spirits appeared in the form of little green elves. The woman apeared first. Her name is Ninopchka. The male appeared second. His name is Pumpernickle. And the little one is named Putchkin. I asked them a question, the answer to which I probably already knew deep down inside. I asked them, 'What do I need most to do to stay well and be healthy?' They said, 'Be happy.' And I asked again, 'What do I need to do to be happy?' And they said, 'Be true to yourself. Be as a child again. Live one day at a time.' Ninopchka said I wouldn't have to give up the ministry as long as I was willing to give her and Putchkin equal time every day. To me, that means getting back to nature, getting back to solitude, and getting back to oneness with the infinite every single day. I agreed to do this and, in return, they promised they'd always be there to guide and counsel me whenever the need arises. To seal the bargain, we all joined hands and did this joyous little dance underneath the trees."

We told her we believe it's more empowering to see
these allies as dream figures generated by the circuitry
of the human brain rather than as disembodied spirits
with an existence of their own. The minister smiled and
said that was fine with her as long as she could dream
them up anytime she liked and, if they were all-knowing
aspects of herself, she was sure she could.

A somber-looking gentleman with a pained expression on his face raised his hand to say, "I'm wondering
about the possible danger of relying entirely on the intuitive process, the female process, when making real-
world decisions."

This question raises an important point. In decision
making, consensus is the key. Once you have input from
each aspect of yourself, it's a good idea, whenever possible, to select a course of action on which all three can
agree. If what you decide to do feels right and makes
sense, you're probably on track. If it also seems like it
might be fun, you can't miss.

"I get the sense that there's a horrendously loud dia-
logue going on within myself," the somber-looking man
went on to say. "It seems as if I can never get to a consensus. I feel like I'm always being pulled in ten different directions. When this happens, nothing I decide to
do turns out right. Is it fair to assume, then, that someone inside is sabotaging things because that someone
isn't being heard enough? Do you think this may have
something to do with the headaches and bouts of depression that have been plaguing me for six years now?"

"Can you see your allies now?" Susan asked him.

"Yes."

"Who's the one that's hollering?"

"The child. He looks like Dennis the Menace throwing a temper tantrum."

"Ask him what he's so mad about. See what comes to mind."

"No one's taking care of him. He always gets ignored."

"Is he the one who's hurting your head and making you sad?"

"Yes."

"Why is he doing that?"

"He says it's to attract my attention."

"Does your head hurt right now?"

"It sure does."

"Now that Dennis has your full attention, ask him what you can do today in return for which he'll stop pounding on your head."

For a while, the somber-looking man was silent. Suddenly, he broke into a broad smile and, then, a hearty laugh. He said Dennis's demands consisted of an ice cream soda, a swim, and a funny movie. Then, his expression clouded over as his male personality, whom he visualized as John Calvin, took charge again. He said this kind of frivolity wasn't feasible because he had too many responsibilities. His female ally, Greta Garbo, agreed. She said that with all the people a minister has to serve, there just aren't enough hours in a day to do everything that has to be done, so doing things just for the fun of it was out of the question for the foreseeable future. So, no soda, no swim, no movie.

"How's your head feeling right now?" we asked.

"There's a jackhammer pounding holes in my skull."

"Would you like to try an experiment?" we asked.

"Due to the circumstances," he said, "I'm willing to try anything."

"Are you willing to try accepting Dennis's terms?"

"Impossible. I've got a newsletter to get out and a sermon to prepare. I've committed myself to working on both of them tonight."

We suggested that with his head feeling the way it did, he probably wouldn't get very far on those projects and that maybe he could negotiate a win-win consensus whereby Dennis would get some fun time and, in return, Calvin could get some of his work done. Calvin said he was willing to stop for an ice cream soda after the seminar and rent a funny video tape if, in return, Dennis would stop pounding on his head and let him get some work done. Dennis said, "Throw in a hot bath, and you've got a deal." Calvin agreed, they shook hands, and immediately, the headache was 85 percent relieved. Dennis said he was keeping the other 15 percent in reserve to make sure the old bastard kept his word. That brought the house down.

Another minister got up to say he now had a new perspective on what Jesus meant when he said you can't enter the kingdom "except ye be as a little child." Then, he shared a prescription for prevention of burnout recommended by humorist James Thurber: "After a little Einstein, there ought to be a little Cole Porter. After talk about Kierkegaard and Kafka should come imitations of Ed Wynn and W. C. Fields. Humor is counterbalance. Laughter need not be cut out of anything since it includes everything."

Burnout has less to do with too much work than it does with too little laughter and not enough play. We asked the ministers what the five who quit had in common. They were all hardworking, dedicated people with a no-nonsense life-style. Like the character in a movie about Russia who said, "I have no time for frivolity; I only have time for truth," each was totally run by his or her masculine personality. A similar mind-set with a capitalist twist might be, "What good's contentment? It doesn't produce income." In the lives of people ensnared in this type of single-mindedness, things that matter to the feminine personality in the right brain (creativity, harmony, beauty) and to the child's mind in the hindbrain (laughing, feeling good, having fun) don't have to take a backseat because they're not even allowed on the bus. Let's draw on your imagination to give you a feel for what it's like to live like this.

Suppose you're doing seventy-seven m.p.h. on a highway with a speed limit of sixty-five. Maybe your inner child is out and enjoying going fast, or maybe your goal-directed ego mind is racing the clock so he can get more and more done in less and less time. In the first case, you're having fun and feeling fine. Happiness hormones (joy juices) secreted by your brain are surging through your body, stimulating a sense of exhilaration. In the second case, you're doing exactly the same thing and feeling awful. Thinking makes the difference. Impatient, worrisome thoughts churned out by the "adulterated" male in your left brain are converted into stress hormones (worry juices), which make you feel anxious, nervous, and tense. A surprising number of people in our culture spend most of their waking hours in this state. No wonder they burn out. Too much worry juice is harmful to your health because, in large doses, it's toxic. It needs to be neutralized every single day. Many people neutralize it with alcohol. Others use drugs. These solutions create their own problems and are nowhere near as effective as a specific antidote: joy juice.

For a dramatic illustration of how potent and fast acting mind-generated hormones are, suppose that in your rearview mirror, you see a car with flashing red lights bearing down on you. You know you're doing twelve miles an hour more than the law allows. Instant adrenaline. Just picturing this scenario, you're probably experiencing a squirt right now. This is because your body reacts to a mental image just as it would to an actual event. To grasp how completely and effectively joy juice neutralizes worry juice, suppose it's your lucky day. The highway patrol, siren screaming, zooms right past you and disappears down the road ahead. Instant relief.

Now, consider this. It's not the image in the rearview mirror that pushes your panic button. It's the belief that it represents someone or something "out there" chasing you. Any image, even a dream, that triggers this belief will get your juices going. One of our phone clients, a surgeon with a successful practice and no time to play, awoke one night in a cold sweat. His heart was pounding, his mouth was dry, he was panting, and his back hurt. He'd been dreaming about being chased by a redneck cop in a green uniform. In the dream, the cop opened the trunk of the doctor's car, saw a broken drum inside, and flew into a rage. A week later, the doctor's back was still hurting. His symptoms had all the earmarks of a slipped disk.

"I'm looking at three unpalatable options," he said when he first called. "Surgery with no guarantee of relief and a high statistical probability that the condition will recur even if the operation is successful. I can use narcotics to control the pain with all that implies addiction-wise, or I can just learn to live with it. It has come to my attention that you may be able to offer me a fourth option, and that's why I'm calling."

The doctor, let's call him Frank, knew that the human brain secretes powerful painkillers, and he was familiar with the mechanism by which visual imagery stimulates that process. What he wanted from us was a technique to make this happen for him. We told him the only pain anyone can relieve is one they've got right now.

"Right now," he said, "I've got an ache in the small of my back I'd sure like to get rid of."

"Can you precisely outline the edges of the ache and determine its three-dimensional shape?" we asked.

After a moment of silence, he decided it was shaped like one of those old-fashioned windup alarm clocks, about three and a half inches in diameter and about an inch and a half thick. It was jammed against his backbone. He said it felt as if the mainspring had herniated through the case, and every time he coughed, sneezed, or moved too quickly, it would come flying out to shoot down the back of his leg and, yes, he could picture it.

Now that he had converted his symptom into a mental image, Frank was ready to take the next step. This involved changing the image and, with it, the symptom. To start the process, he imagined that with his in breath, he could draw a wave of vibratory energy—ultrasound—up the front of his body to the top of his head. Then, as he was exhaling, he imagined the ultrasound energy sliding down his backbone and swirling around the clock with the exploding mainspring. He told us he could actually feel it doing this. At the same time, he pictured the imaginary alarm clock disintegrating and melting under the influence of the high-frequency energy engulfing and penetrating it. As Frank completed each exhalation, he imagined the energy running down the backs of his legs, through his heels, and into the ground, carrying bits and pieces of shattered case and clockwork with it. The ground acted as a filter, removing the debris as a fresh wave of pure energy traveled up the front of Frank's body with his next inhalation. Pretty soon, the imaginary clock was gone, and so was the ache.

Two days later, Frank called back to say he was no longer in constant pain. "Any time it starts, I can make it stop. I can also get to the bathroom and back with a lot less trouble. I really appreciate this, because I especially hate using a bedpan. Humiliating as hell. I presume the process stimulates secretion of endorphins and cortisones by the hindbrain. This would explain relief

161

of pain and what feels like markedly decreased swelling and inflammation in the tissues around the herniated disk. I'm wondering if it might also induce disintegration and resorption of the extruded cartilage. I'd like that a lot better than having to have it repaired surgically."

"If you believe it can," we said, "it might. If you believe it can't, it won't."

Frank laughed and told us about one of his neighbors who can cure warts. But only for those who believe he can. "He rubs it with the middle finger of his left hand while silently running a particular Bible verse through his mind. If the patient has one hundred percent faith in his ability, the wart disappears within a week. If he sees the slightest flicker of doubt in the patient's eyes, he won't even try. I know it works because he disappeared a plantar wart from my wife's foot. You know how tough they can be. She's metaphysically oriented and believes anything is possible if you put your mind to it. So she just decided to believe it would work and it did. He wouldn't say which Bible verse he uses because he was afraid she might try it on a nonbeliever. Actually, it wouldn't work, and that would make him look bad."

Frank said he was willing to try anything as long as it made sense. "I can see how belief and images of disappearing warts conjured up by the patient can activate his or her immune system so that it attacks and destroys the lesion. Likewise, I can see how the imagery you taught me can activate my chondroclasts [cartilage-dissolving cells]. I'm willing to devote the next six weeks to seeing if I can make that happen. The possibility that I might have to submit to invasive surgery as a last resort is bound to keep my nose to the grindstone. The problem is that, statistically, this thing has a high probability of recurrence. So even if I clear it up, by whatever means, I still need a way to make sure it doesn't happen again."

This got us talking about looking at Frank's bad back in terms of purpose rather than cause. We asked what it was forcing him to do that he would never allow himself to do if he didn't have it.

"That's easy," he said. "It has made me take six weeks off from work. With all the responsibilities I have to keep up with on a daily basis, I hardly have time to go to the bathroom, let alone take a vacation. My last one was six years ago—a three-day weekend. I tell you, it feels as if I still haven't caught up from that one. I know I can get other surgeons to cover for me. I had to do that because of this back thing. But how could I relax and enjoy myself knowing that if they screw up it's my responsibility? Just thinking about it is giving me a pain in the butt. Maybe I'm just burned out from an overload of stress hormones. My wife says if I get the message from this episode the universe won't have to deck me again to teach me the same lesson. She tells me to think about how often I find myself operating on the same patients for different reasons, like an auto repairman who fixes a car that's been run into a telephone pole only to have the driver take it out and run it into something else, time and time again."

So what do a dream about an angry policeman and a broken drum, six weeks of forced retirement and the image of an alarm clock with a herniated mainspring have in common? They were all clues pointing to the connection between Frank's bad back and his workaholic life-style. As we chatted on the telephone, Frank dreamed up a fantasy that put it all together.

He imagined himself up in a tree house where he used to spend a lot of time as a boy. Watching the images in his mind the way one watches the pictures on a TV screen, he saw Peter Pan, dressed like the policeman in the dream about the broken drum, fly into the tree and sit down, facing him. Then, Mr. Spock, first officer of the *Starship Enterprise*, materialized on his left, and Cher, singer, actress, and TV personality, appeared on his right. Frank imagined himself asking each of the others if they had jammed the alarm clock into his spine and sprung the mainspring.

Peter stood up, took a bow, and said, "I cannot tell a lie. It was I."

"Why?" Frank asked.

"Because he broke my drum," Peter answered, pointing a finger at Mr. Spock, who shrugged and said it was necessary. "He never lets us play," Peter went on. "So we fixed it so he can't work."

At this point in the daydream, Frank got a flash of insight. He remembered drumming. As a child, he did it all the time. For his twelfth birthday, his parents got him a drum set, and he took to spending hour after hour in the basement, playing along with phonograph records and with the radio. About five years later, he started a small band that played at high school dances, parties, and other social occasions. The group was good, so they were popular and able to earn money doing what they loved to do. For the next few years, Frank was happy as a clam. His inner child, Peter, got to bang away at the drums to his heart's content, and his creative, feminine aspect, represented by Cher, loved everything about show business, espccially being up on stage.

Then, one thing led to another, and Frank applied to medical school. The day he got his letter of acceptance, his rational mind, the Spock in him, took charge, and everything changed. He decided that hanging out with musicians and making a public spectacle of himself was inappropriate behavior for a physician. Besides, studying medicine was a full-time occupation that left no time for anything else. As a concession, Spock agreed it would be okay to keep on drumming, but only as a hobby to be practiced in his spare time, if he could find any. He selected surgcry as a specialty because it required meticulous attention to detail and because he liked fixing things.

So, as workaholics do, Frank disowned and abandoned two-thirds of his being (Cher and Peter) and totally identified with his ego, the doctor (Spock). As a result, he became a voluntary slave to what psychoanalyst Karen Horney called "the tyranny of the shoulds." Spock was a perfectionist whose motto was, "If you want it done right, you should do it yourself." He spent all his time slogging through mountains of chores he believed should

165

get done and done right in order to meet his professional responsibilities. His wife said the mountains were creations of his own mind, and if he didn't stop "shoulding all over yourself" pretty soon, something was bound to give. She was right. It did.

One evening, Frank was down in the basement looking for a back issue of a medical journal and noticed his drums sitting in a corner gathering dust. Spock decided that the space they were taking could be put to better use as a storage area for his rapidly expanding collection of medical journals. He decided he would make arrangements to have the drum set removed and disposed of first thing in the morning. Then, he found what he was looking for and took it up to read in bed. That night, he had the dream about the broken drum and woke up with excruciating pain in the small of his back.

"I had no inkling that there might be a connection between my decision to dispose of the drums and this back problem. I thought it was precipitated by jockeying those heavy cartons around trying to get at the journal I was after."

"Maybe," we theorized, "that was just the last straw — the one that broke the camel's back, so to speak. Apparently, you've been actively engaged in inner child abuse for a long time. Considering your experience in terms of the allegory you just dreamed up, we could say Spock's decision to trash Peter's drums and replace them with medical journals went over the line. What do you imagine Peter would say about that?"

"Damn right!" Frank said.

166

"So if you want your disk to heal and stay healed, you might think about reordering your priorities. In other words," we suggested, "Spock is going to have to look at making concessions to Peter. He'll only do this if he gets something he wants in return. Ask Peter what his price is for giving you enough pain-free mobility to get you to the bathroom and back all day today so you don't have to use a bedpan."

"Can he really do that?" Frank wanted to know.

"Strike a bargain and see," we said. "He represents the mind in your hindbrain, which, as you know, does run your body."

Spock saw the logic in that and agreed to negotiate. He also said he never realized Peter had that much power. It struck Frank that his disability presented an opportunity to get back into drumming. Peter said he'd restore Frank's bathroom privileges on condition that he spend some time today playing along with the radio the way he used to when he was a teenager—just for fun. Spock agreed that, under the circumstances, this kind of frivolity was allowable and, if it could lead to his release from bondage to the bedpan, even desirable. Frank asked his wife if she would mind fetching his drumsticks and practice pad from the basement.

"It's about time," she said. "If getting knocked off your feet is making you play again, I would say it's a blessing in disguise."

A practice pad is a square of wood, about half an inch thick, with a facing of hard rubber. It's designed to let drummers practice without making a racket. Frank's rented hospital bed was cranked up to support his back in an upright position as he happily tapped out rhythms in time to the tunes pouring into his head through a set of stereophonic earphones. He had such a good time practicing drumming instead of medicine that he forgot about the professional journals he'd been forcing himself to read for at least two hours every day.

Peter kept his end of the bargain and turned the tables on Spock by stating that if he wanted to continue bathroom privileges he'd have to use that time drumming instead of reading doctor stuff. Spock fussed at first, but faced with return to the bedpan, he reluctantly agreed. Frank's wife reinforced the bargain by removing all traces of medical literature from the bedroom and by announcing that the only reading material she was willing to carry upstairs would be fiction, nonprofessional publications, or books and magazines about music. On this regime, joy juices neutralized and replaced the stress hormones that had weakened Frank's body and allowed it to break down. Every day, in every way, he was feeling better and better.

After about a week, Spock tried to break the agreement and reassert his authority. Frank had just set up the practice pad when he decided he was falling too far behind in his required reading program, and this time would be better spent catching up. He was alone in the house and thought he'd seize the opportunity to sneak downstairs, retrieve a journal or two, and smuggle them into the bedroom. As soon as he set foot on the floor, a searing pain exploded in the small of his back and shot down his leg as far as the ankle. It was all he could do to crawl back into bed. Only after an intense session of visualizing dissolving the herniated mainspring and promising himself never to try anything like that again, did it let up. But it took a while.

After three weeks of forced idleness (lying around in bed all day, watching television, and listening to music and drumming on his practice pad), Frank was ready for the next step on the road to recovery. Peter agreed to allow him to maneuver up and down the stairs on condition that he dust off his drums and spend some time playing them every day. Doing this rekindled an old flame. Frank remembered how much he had always loved making music and became acutely aware of how much he still did.

Six weeks after he hurt his back, Frank was well again but not the way he was before. Along with the disk, the musician in him had herniated and was demanding equal time with his ego, the doctor. Neither could be stuffed or ignored. Now, he had to find a balance between what he felt like doing and what he thought he should be doing.

Logically, he thought he should set the drums aside and get back into harness. Just contemplating that possibility, he could feel his back stiffen—an early warning signal from Peter to Spock. Images of people running automobiles into telephone poles flashed through Frank's mind. He knew he was flirting with the possibility of chronic disability and/or multiple surgeries. It struck him that he could give up his practice and get back into music full-time. This set off a blast of energy in his belly and chest. He couldn't tell if it was pure joy, stark terror, or a combination of both.

Caught between a rock and a hard place, Frank found a way out through a daydream. He called a meeting of his allies in the tree house. Since the argument was between Spock and Peter, his feminine ally, portrayed by Cher, played the part of mediator. Her views were similar to those of Sylvia, Frank's wife. Like a pair of horse traders at a country fair, where one says, "I wouldn't touch that flea-bitten bag of dog food with a ten foot pole," and the other says, "I wouldn't sell my Nellie to you if you were the last person on earth," Spock and Peter's opening positions were poles apart. Now that he was up and about again, Spock was determined to get right back on the treadmill and work even harder to make up for lost time. Peter was just as determined to do whatever it would take to get Frank back into music, full-time. Starting with the opening scene, Frank dreamed up a happy ending to his inner play, which changed his life.

Cher pointed out that without a healthy body, Frank couldn't maintain a surgical practice no matter how hard he was willing to work. Spock saw the logic and admitted that just as he had to negotiate to get well, he now had to negotiate to stay well. Repeating Sylvia's words, Cher noted that he had just taken six weeks off and the world hadn't come to an end or even missed a beat. Frank's receptionist had managed to keep the office functional and the bills paid, and to refer Frank's patients to two colleagues who cared for them competently and efficiently during his absence. "You could have been on vacation all this time, and things would have worked out just as well," Cher said. "Maybe if you did that voluntarily, once a year, Peter wouldn't have to knock you flat on your back to get his playtime."

"Damn right!" Peter said. "But it's not enough. Throw in three days off every week and four hours of playtime every workday and you've got a deal."

Spock turned green. Frank felt another surge of terror/joy in his chest. It was as though the energy locked in his back had broken loose and was moving up and out. After some haggling, Spock finally agreed to a five-day workweek with two hours set aside for music making each day and a guaranteed six-week annual vacation in return for a pain-free, fully functional back.

Spock said he couldn't see how he could give up that much control and still survive. Cher said he didn't have to. He could just transform.

The fantasy figures we meet in our dreams, night or day, are like the people we meet in time and space. You never know what they're likely to do next. So, even though he knew he was making it all up, Frank was surprised to see Spock stand up, walk to the end of the platform, and, without a word, jump over the edge. He was even more surprised to see Spock hit the ground and bounce back into the tree house as the Reverend Albert Schweitzer, M.D., a minister turned physician whose autobiography was a key factor in Frank's decision to study medicine. His guiding ethical principle was "Reverence for Life." After that, everything changed.

Frank rebalanced his life so that each of his three aspects would have equal time. To honor the commitment he'd made to himself in a daydream as insurance against recurrence of the back problem, Frank took in a partner and restructured his practice so there was enough time to make music, nurture his relationship with Sylvia, and serve his patients. As part of this service, he now checks each patient's "serum fun level" by asking them what they love to do and advising them to make sure they do it on a regular basis.

Sometime later, at a music festival, Frank met a producer who was planning a documentary on music and medicine for British television. Before the evening was over, Frank had agreed to sign on to the project as a consultant. "I'm still practicing medicine," he wrote us. "In this lifetime, that's what I know I'm supposed to be doing. Only, now, what I do is in tune with who I am, a music maker. I make a lot less money, but I'm having more fun. I consider that an acceptable trade-off. Especially in light of the fact that my back is working fine. No sign of the dreaded recurrence. I guess I've learned how to steer around telephone poles. I'm on sabbatical from my practice back in the states, and I'm not sure if I'll ever go back to slaving over a hot operating table again. No one 'in here' seems at all interested in doing that. Sylvia is helping me live one day at a time, and I must say, so far, so good. Right now, everything's good. And, as I see it, right now is all there is."

The common thread connecting these stories is transformation. Total, irreversible life change. Psychologically, it involves dying to be reborn. To many people, this is scary business. Let's take a closer look at the process and at ways of easing the transition by converting panic into joy.

11

Over the Edge

What the caterpillar calls a disaster,
the master calls a butterfly.
RICHARD BACH

Two caterpillars are socializing on a rock when a butterfly happens to fly by.

"Did you see that?" says one.

"I tell you," says the other. "You'll never catch me up in one of them things!"

Not far away, standing at the edge of a cliff, a person was watching the same butterfly. Suddenly, the ground gave way under her feet. Then, after a hundred meter free fall, she brushed against a rope attached to a tree stump, grabbed it, and held on for dear life. Looking down, she saw there was still a long way to go. So she looked up and yelled as loud as she could. "Is anyone up there?"

The clouds parted, and a shaft of golden light descended to envelop her. Also emanating from the heavens above came a thunderous voice: "I'M UP HERE!"

"Can you help me?"

"WILL YOU OBEY MY COMMANDMENT WITH-OUT QUESTION?"

"What do you want me to do?"

"LET GO OF THE ROPE!"

For a long time, she just hung there, thinking about

that. Then, she looked up again. "Is there anyone else up there?"

When you reach the end of your rope and there's no one around to help, your choices are limited and your reactions predictable. Naturally, you hang on as long as possible and when you can't hang on any longer, you let go. This is what happened to our lady from the top of the cliff. The rope slipped through her fingers, and down she went, kicking and screaming. After what seemed like a lifetime, she hit bottom and the falling stopped. All she was aware of was total, absolute silence. Feeling no pain, she opened her eyes and looked around. A shaft of golden sunlight was streaming in through her bedroom window, enveloping and warming her. The alarm clock on her nightstand was beeping.

Charlie pushed the bar that activates the ten-minute nap cycle, settled back, and idly watched the thoughts floating around in her mind. "What a weird dream. Sure seemed real. As if I just dropped out of another world into this one. Shamans do that—leave their bodies and travel to other worlds to meet spirit guides and get advice how to live in this one. A couple of caterpillars, a butterfly, and God. An odd assortment of guides. Wonder what it all means." Then, she dozed. When the alarm sounded again, she turned it off, put the whole thing out of her mind, and got ready to start day one of her new job.

Charlie was a chemical engineer with a giant corporation. After nine years on the job, she got promoted—from insecticides and weed killers to product development.

More money, full charge of a state-of-the-art lab, and a private office with her name on the door. A gratifying step up the corporate ladder, especially for a woman. Charlie figured she had it made. At least her ego, the chemical engineer, did. But there was a fly in the ointment.

The laboratory she was now heading was set up to research and develop a new nerve gas for the Pentagon. Charlie had no problem with that until the evening of the first day on the job. Driving home, she heard a news report on the car radio. It was about a dictator in the Middle East using chemical weapons to subdue an unruly population. The reporter talked about whole families being wiped out in their own homes by clouds of poison gas. There were no pictures. Charlie didn't need any. She knew enough about the stuff to convert the reporter's words about what was happening in those villages into graphic mental images. They danced around in her head like a tune you can't get out of your mind and brought her face-to-face with the consequences of what she was now doing to earn a living. She felt like she did in the dream when the ground gave way under her feet.

Psychologically, Charlie was in early labor. After nine years comfortably cradled in the corporate womb, she was experiencing guilt pangs, which, like labor pains, were coming in waves and threatening to force her out. This set off a royal battle in Charlie's psyche: reason and logic against emotionally charged images. Her rational, security-oriented inner male saw no reason to let go of the job. And he made a very convincing argument for hanging on.

"It took almost twenty years of hard work to get to this point. Why throw it away just when it's starting to pay off? It doesn't make sense. Quitting this job won't put an end to chemical warfare. What it will put an end to is financial security, medical insurance, and a pension plan I've been paying into for almost ten years." The image of women and children writhing in agony and gasping for breath flashed through Charlie's mind. In response, the security-oriented intellect in her left brain came up with the classical argument of the professional executioner. "Quitting this job," she reasoned, "won't save a single life. If I don't do this, someone else will. Then, I'll be out in the cold with nothing but high-minded principles to keep me warm. Ethical principles and social conscience are fine as far as they go, but the fact is, they don't pay the rent or put food on the table. I'd be out of a job, and nothing else would change. What a waste."

Charlie was convinced and decided to do the sensible thing: hang on to the job. For the next few months, all went well. The story that upset her dropped out of the news, and she didn't think about it anymore. Then, she went to a party and heard a joke.

A priest, a doctor, and an arms merchant were out deep-sea fishing. On the way back to port, their boat sprang a leak and sank. Luckily, there was a large rock outcropping about one hundred yards from where the boat went down. All three managed to reach it and climb up. Then, they noticed the tide was coming in. It was only a matter of time before they'd be back in the drink.

They thought they might try swimming the mile or so to shore, but a great white shark was circling the rock, eyeing them hungrily. The arms merchant volunteered to jump into the water and distract the shark while the other two tried to swim to safety. As soon as he hit the water, the shark made a beeline for the arms merchant. It dove, picked him up on its back, swam to shore, and, with a flip of its tail, tossed him onto the beach.

"Did you see that?" said the priest. "It's a miracle!"

"No miracle, Padre," said the doctor. "Professional courtesy."

Charlie said she didn't appreciate being the butt of moronic jokes and left the party in a huff. The person who told the story had no idea what line of work she was in, so her reaction was irrational to the point of paranoia. Charlie realized this before she was ten minutes out the door. But then, you can't reason with guilt pangs any more than you can with labor pains. Stage one (active labor) of Charlie's ongoing birth process shifted into high gear as the image maker in her right brain, the feminine side, increased the pressure. The engineer drove home, went to bed, and had a nightmare about sharks slashing people and gobbling up gold coins that poured out of the victims' wounds along with their blood. The dream woke her up and kept her up all night. She couldn't get it out of her mind for days.

Then, the dictator who gassed his own people invaded a neighboring country. When the enemy counterattacked, he hit them with chemical weapons. Once again, Charlie found herself listening to detailed descriptions of the suffering inflicted on real people by substances she was actively involved in creating. This time, the casualties were seventeen- and eighteen-year-old boys drafted into the army to help repel the invader. Some were said to be as young as fifteen. Charlie had a fifteen-year-old son. The day she heard these news reports, she was in her office trying to iron out a kink in the production process. Suddenly, she saw an image of her own son as a victim of the end product of that process and had to take the rest of the day off. Her ego, the engineer, was determined to hang onto this job no matter what. So he fought back with antidepressants, tranquilizers, and sleeping pills. The drugs had the effect the doctors said they would. They suppressed the troublesome images and, along with that, Charlie's ability to concentrate. So, for her security-oriented inner male, that gamut was a net loss. There was nothing he could do to stave off the inevitable. Stage two of the birth process, expulsion from the womb, happened suddenly and unexpectedly. Here's how she tells it.

"The plant supervisor and I were discussing a design problem. Before I could stop myself, I heard myself telling him that for reasons of conscience, I might have to quit. Part of me was appalled. This part knew I was burning my bridges behind me. Another part of me, a part I hadn't been willing to recognize, had taken over and was out of control. Before I could rein it back in, I was out of a job. Then, the other shoe dropped. I asked if I could go back to insecticides and weed killers and was told that, due to defense cutbacks, the company was retrenching and my old position had been eliminated. What's more, there was a hiring freeze so there were no openings in any other department. And that was that."

As she was clearing out her desk, Charlie got the strong feeling that she'd done this exact same thing once before. She just couldn't remember where or when. Then, she noticed the calendar and realized it was her birthday. When a primary life support system comes unglued like this, transformation is the key to survival. So that's what Charlie did. She transformed the nine-to-five working chemist into a company president/creative artist. Drawing on business contacts formed over the past fifteen years, she created her own corporation—a consultation service for companies looking to get out of the arms business and into ecologically sound, consumer-oriented products. The time was right, and her business flourished. She made lots of money and was able to get back into oil painting—something she loved to do but had never been able to find time for. All of which proves that EVERY ENDING IS A NEW BEGINNING.

When it feels as if the ground has dropped out from under your feet, it's nice to know this. But by itself, it's not enough. We need a way to handle the explosion of emotional energy that erupts when life's support systems disintegrate. Some people scurry around trying to put things back together and make them be the way they were before. You might as well try to tack a detached placenta back into place.

Buddha said the source of all human suffering is

attachment. That would include attachment to ropes we come to the end of. Letting go is scary, so we hang on even though it hurts. What keeps people tied into painful attitudes, relationships, and stressful situations is fear of the unknown. The next time you've got to let go of a rope (job, relationship, a way of life), remember that scary as it seems at the time, you never know how it's going to end up. Consider the possibility that what looks like a disaster while it's happening might turn out to be a blessing in disguise.

The first rope you had to let go of was your umbilical cord, after free fall through the birth canal dropped you into a bright new world. Actually, who you were before you were born was an underwater plant. Growing at the end of a stem attached to a root system buried in the wall of the womb, you had everything you could possibly need. Total perfection. Absolute bliss. Then, it was birthday. Someone or something pulled the plug, and your warm, cuddly world came to a violent end. The waters ran out, the muscles that once protected you squeezed down, and out you went, kicking and screaming. Your life support system was ripped up by the roots and dropped away. For the one going through it, this series of events hardly seems like cause for celebration. Obviously you survived, because here you are, years later, reading about it. For you, the fetus, it was a disaster. The end of a world. For you, the infant, it was the beginning of a new life. Changing doesn't end with physical birth. Waiting in the wings are puberty, maturity, and aging.

Over the Edge

In time, every stage of life, even life itself, becomes another rope we have to let go of. People who've had a close brush with death and gotten a glimpse of the other side tell us that human life ends the way it begins. Free fall through a long, dark tunnel into a dazzling white light. What they experienced at the end of this life and beyond that tunnel was unadulterated ecstasy. Being dead is okay, they say. Dying is the problem. What makes it a problem is fear—fear of change.

Scientist/astronaut Brian O'Leary told an audience at the University of California at Santa Cruz, "Life on our planet is now undergoing a change which is comparable to what happened when the first living creatures crawled out of the sea to establish themselves on dry land."

The more things change, the more they remain the same. Forever changing. Changing, transformation, has two sides: death and birth. You can't have one without the other. Nowadays, things are changing faster than ever before, and the pace is increasing rapidly. Everything old is dying. Something new is being born. Whether this is cause for celebration or alarm depends on your attitude. Attitudes are points of view programmed into the left brain at an early age. They organize perceptions into emotional experiences and come in two basic varieties: pessimistic and optimistic. The pessimist agonizes over the death of the fetus. The optimist celebrates the birth of the child. The following anecdote shows how opposing attitudes can structure a single event into two totally different life experiences.

183

While her kids were away for the weekend, Mrs. Jones spread a load of horse manure over her lawn to fertilize it. When he got home and realized what the lawn was full of, the older boy burst into tears. He was sure that mean, bad people did it because they hated him and his family and wanted to make them feel bad. Squealing with delight, the other child ran into the garage, down to the basement, and hunted through every room of the house. "With all that doo doo on the lawn," she said, "there's got to be a pony around here someplace."

Everything else being equal, which of these two kids do you expect might live longer? Or have a happier life? Which reflects your attitude toward change?

Trying to make change stop is counterproductive. The harder you try, the worse it gets. You might as well try to make the world stop spinning. Ignoring change, the way Brenda and Bert do, doesn't work either.

One day, they rented a rowboat and went fishing. They found a great spot and pulled them in one after another. When they'd reached the legal limit, Brenda suggested they mark the spot so they could come back tomorrow for more. Bert thought that was a great idea. He pulled a marking crayon out of his pocket and made an **X** on the seat he was sitting on and another on the seat Brenda was fishing from.

"Tomorrow when we come back," he said, "I'll fish from here and you fish from right there."

"Great idea, dearie," said Brenda. "But how do you know we'll get the same boat tomorrow?"

Trying to live life without taking change into account

is silly. Trying to make it stop is self-destructive. So maybe we could learn to live with it, even enjoy it. That's easier to do if we have a handle on how it works. It's probably safe to say the most radical change you've been through in this life happened on your birthday. You got through that by doing what was necessary without thinking about it. And now that you can think about it, you might consider that it happened in three stages: (1) escalating pressure, (2) expulsion from the womb, and (3) separation of a primary life-support system.

That's the letting go phase. The scary part. Next comes transformation. Fetus into infant, caterpillar into butterfly. Getting through the scary part is a lot easier if you know how to handle anxiety. We recommend the three-pronged approach: (1) Program the thinker in the left brain to recognize anxiety for what it is—free energy. (2) Induce the computerized pharmacy in the hindbrain to secrete natural tranquilizers that calm you so that you can effectively use the energy released. (3) Tap into the life guidance circuitry in the right brain through a daydream. After a brief discussion designed to help you see your emotions in a new light, we'll put together a composite case history from the files of the Transformational Learning Center to show how the process works in actual practice.

Many people scream when they ride a roller coaster. More often than not, even the screamer doesn't know for sure whether these are screams of terror or screams of joy. Just by listening, you can't tell one from the other. People scream at horror movies, too. There's no doubt that these are screams of terror. Since they're willing to pay for the experience, it's obvious that billions of people enjoy feeling terror—which would lead us to believe that terror and joy are related. Dr. Hans Selye, who made medical history by showing how stress affects living creatures, told us there is reason to believe that, like birth and death, joy and panic are the two faces of a single event.

Suppose two politicians, on opposite sides of a bloody civil war, are in different parts of town, watching the same newscast. Rebel forces have surrounded the city and are about to take it over. One panics; the other jumps for joy. At the height of this reaction, doctors perform a physical examination including a blood test on each and record the findings. They send these findings to the finest medical institutions in the world and ask the most gifted professionals on staff to decide, on the basis of those findings, which patient was in a state of panic and which was experiencing ecstatic joy. They can't because the reports are pretty much the same. Each describes a person in a state of excitement induced by high levels of adrenaline in the blood.

Suppose now that we carry our hypothetical study a step further by injecting each of a pair of identical twins with the same amount of adrenaline. Then, as the drug takes effect, we ask one to watch the nightly news while the other watches a performance by a talented comic. The first will experience the adrenaline rush as an anxiety attack, while the second will react with a wave of joyous exhilaration. The same drug, contrasting emotions.

The factor making the difference must have been the subjects' states of mind. The effects of adrenaline are predictable and constant. It sets off a charge of energy in the physical body that throws it into a state of arousal or excitement. The word *emotion* means outward movement. What moves out is this charge of raw chemical energy. When we feel it, we label it and give it names like lust, anger, joy, anxiety, or whatever. The names we choose reflect the thoughts and mental images that happen to be going through our minds when the energy rises.

Any one of an infinite variety of triggers can set off the charge. The specific one we've been discussing here is change. Many people view change, and disruption of familiar patterns, with alarm. The alarm reaction is mediated by adrenaline and experienced as anxiety. Like all emotions, anxiety is, among other things, a bodily state. Like Frank, the surgeon in the last chapter, you can convert it into a mental image and "disappear" it by changing the image. One of our clients, let's call him Harvey, was able to dispel the mental anguish of midlife crisis by dealing with its manifestation in his physical body.

After twenty-five years, Harvey's marriage fell apart. It didn't fail. It just fell apart. If the purpose of a marriage is to produce children and provide an environment for them to grow up in, Harvey's was successful. Splitting apart like a ripe fruit, it fulfilled itself as family members, like seeds, scattered to take root and grow on their own.

After hanging on as long as he could, Harvey eventually

accepted the inevitable. Divorce. Getting the final papers threw him into an identity crisis. He felt like a character out of one of the cartoons his kids used to watch Saturday morning—like the cat who runs ten feet off the edge of a cliff and for a while just hangs there, suspended in midair. Caught between an irretrievable past and inconceivable future, he asked himself, "If I'm not a husband or a father anymore, then who the hell am I?"

When he first came to see us, Harvey was feeling awful—too agitated to rest and too exhausted to do anything else. Unable to sleep, he'd been pacing the floor for days. His doctor had prescribed tranquilizers and sleeping pills, which helped some. But when they wore off, he felt worse than before. Obviously, popping pills wasn't the answer. He said if he couldn't get a handle on this real soon, he was sure to go crazy.

When he showed up for his first session, Harvey was up to his ears in what Carl Jung called "a cramp of consciousness." The thinker in his left brain was completely out of control. He couldn't turn it off. Thoughts were racing around in his mind like a bunch of drunken monkeys in a cage. They just wouldn't stop. Thoughts about the past depressed him. Thoughts about the future agitated him. To go with his heavy heart, he developed a nervous stomach. Other thoughts triggered feelings of disbelief, hope, anger, frustration, and despair. No wonder he felt as if he was going crazy.

Being a left-brained scientist, Harvey was accustomed to using logical analysis to solve his problems: (1) Identify the problem. (2) Isolate the cause. (3) Remove it.

Unfortunately, as he found out, for problems in relationships, this approach doesn't work too well. But it did come in handy for dealing with his agitated depression.

Step 1, identifying the problem, was easy. An explosion of emotion was disrupting his body and unhinging his mind. Step 2, isolating the cause, took discrimination. At first glance, you might think it was the divorce, but it wasn't. That was just the trigger. Any one of a wide variety of triggers could have set it off. What was keeping it going and driving him crazy was the act of thinking. Step 3 boiled down to finding the answer to a simple question: How do you stop thinking?

This question may be simple, but the answer isn't—which is why there are so many gadgets and gimmicks around to distract people from their own thoughts. TV, sex, sports, loud music, and an impressive array of chemical agents, to name just a few. None of the above worked for Harvey, so we recommended a technique that blends Eastern spiritual practice and Western scientific know-how. The idea is that watching thoughts instead of thinking them makes them stop. Also, that thinking numbers instead of words while watching yourself breathe gets the brain to secrete natural tranquilizers that relax the body and calm the mind.

As a point of reference, we asked Harvey how he was feeling, right now, on a scale of one to ten. Ten for wonderful, zero for the worst he'd ever felt. He said he was feeling better than he had been. "Maybe minus two." Then we showed him a way to get higher on the feeling scale. You might like to try this yourself.

Focus on your breathing. Inhale for a slow count to five or whatever number you reach when your lungs feel comfortably full. Hold your breath for a count of one or two, whichever feels better. Slowly exhale for a count of five or whatever number you reach when your lungs are comfortably empty. Hold for another count of one or two and repeat the cycle. If a thought should enter your mind, don't get involved with it. Just watch it go by. Picturing yourself in a beautiful place or listening to soft music boosts the process and gets your brain to secrete even more tranquilizers. Next time you find yourself frustrated or worrying about something you can't do anything about, instead of spinning your wheels, take some time out to try this procedure. It could change your life.

After ten minutes of counting and watching himself breathe, Harvey's sense of well-being went up from minus two to plus four. The jangling thoughts were gone, but he was exhausted and unsure about what to do next. Sleep seemed like a good idea, so he went home, practiced keeping his thinker shut down, and slept like a baby. The next day, on a scale of one to ten, he was up around eight. The only thing he did that was different was learn to turn off his thinker.

This time, Harvey was ready for phase two of his rehabilitation program, activating the life-guidance mechanism programmed into the circuitry of his right brain. He began by picturing himself on the porch of a cabin by a lake in the woods. He was sitting in a chair, counting and watching himself breathe. With his mind's eye,

he casually looked around expecting to see a living creature. Walking up the path from the lake, he saw his
grandma. He imagined her giving him a hug and saying
how glad she was to see him again. It occurred to Harvey that he might now be communicating with the
spirit of a relative who had been dead for twenty years.

"No spirit," we told him. "Just a fantasy figure in a
daydream. If you want to get technical, you can say it's
a hologram generated by the circuitry of your right brain.
While you're breathing out, imagine yourself asking if
she's got any advice for you. Watch the thoughts that
come into your mind while you're breathing in."

Something grandma said to him when he was a kid
popped into his mind. "You only make this trip once,
so you might as well enjoy the scenery. To do this, you
have to pay attention to what's happening right now.
Living in the past is like riding backward on a horse.
All you get to see of life is your horse's behind and an
endless trail of horse manure."

"So what should I do now?" he imagined himself asking her on his next out breath.

What came to him on his next in breath really surprised him.

"Take a vacation. The change of scenery will do you
good. You can't play a new game on the old board. Go
some place nice. Tahiti maybe."

Harvey decided to follow his own advice, take a sabbatical and spend a year living and painting in Tahiti
just like Paul Gauguin—something he'd always wanted
to do but never could find the time for. Not long after

191

he got there, he met a wonderful woman, remarried, and lived happily ever after. At least, that's what he was doing at the time of this writing.

Like the lady on the cliff who was watching the butterfly, neither Harvey nor Charlie had a choice. They all fell into free fall by accident. Skydivers do it deliberately. They jump. That propels them into a physical experience of rapidly accelerated change as gravity makes them fall faster and faster. They feel it in their bodies. Then, when they assume the right attitude, the spread-eagle position, their resistance cradles them and slows the rate of fall.

This demonstrates a fundamental fact of life. If you take the leap of faith (let go of the rope) with the right attitude (expectant optimism), the universe supports you. We all need something to assure a soft landing. For the skydiver, that's a parachute. For the rest of us, it's adaptability—the willingness to change.

12

Fables for the Mind's Eye

*It is not possible to solve a problem
at the level of the problem.*
ALBERT EINSTEIN

A long time ago, there was a storyteller named Aesop. His fables, which always had a moral, were about animals who behaved like people. Being a slave, he had to use this "If the shoe fits, wear it" approach to guiding his masters because he knew they wouldn't react well to direct criticism from the likes of him.

One of Aesop's fables is about a dog who's trotting across a bridge on his way home to bury a big bone he just found. About halfway across, he stops to relieve himself against a post and happens to look down at the surface of the river. Looking up at him, he sees what appears to be another dog with a bigger bone. In a flash, he drops the one he has and lets it sink to the bottom as he leaps on the other dog, determined to have the bigger bone for his own. Actually, all he gets for his trouble is soaking wet. The point of the story, what Aesop called the moral, is that people who aren't satisfied with what they've got, and want what someone else has got because they think it's better, run the risk of winding up with nothing.

Like a myth or a fairy tale, this story is an allegory—a sugarcoated lesson in the art of living. Whether or not it actually happened is unimportant. What is important is that it makes us aware of a pattern of behavior any one of us can fall into if we are not paying attention. The fairy tale about the emperor's new clothes falls into the same category. It's not about an actual emperor who was conned by a pair of conniving clothing designers, but about how looking at the world through the eyes of a child can keep this from happening to you. Likewise, the story of the ugly duckling isn't a historical account of an actual event. It's a nice way of comforting people who feel they are being picked on because they are different by letting them know it might be because they are swans among ducks. It has really been interesting for us to see how good that idea can make people feel. The daydreams our clients dream up for themselves do the same. Like custom-tailored myths, they give people insight into their immediate life situation along with specific guidance about what they need to do to improve it.

Once upon a time, there was a beautiful princess whose father, the king, gave her a golden frisbee for her eighteenth birthday. She ran into the garden to try it out and, with the first toss, a gust of wind caught it and carried it up to the highest branches of a tall tree, where it got stuck. As she stood there, wondering what to do next, Big Red, the mangy tomcat who lived in the kitchen, sauntered over and offered to climb up and get it for her if she would let him sleep in her bed that night. The princess said okay and, in the morning, in bed beside her, instead of a mangy tomcat, she found a handsome young prince. He said he'd been turned into a cat by a wicked witch because he wouldn't marry her.

"You're beautiful," said the princess. "Let's get married and live happily ever after."

"Sure," said the prince. "But I bet you're sorry now you had me fixed."

MORAL: TODAY'S PROBLEMS ARE YESTERDAY'S SOLUTIONS.

The client who told it to us said the moral of that story was the story of his life. All through high school, he said he was "horny, lonely, and confused." His parents said the ideal solution for his situation would be to find a nice girl, get married, and settle down. So, after graduation, that is what he did.

Now, he was faced with the problem of earning a living to support a family. His mom and dad had a solution for that, too. They put him through law school and, after he passed his bar exam, set him up in practice. Then, along with regular living expenses, he had to deal with office rent, salaries for a receptionist and a secretary, and payments on a new car. All of which, he was told, were absolutely essential if he was to project the proper image for a professional person. The next item on the agenda was generating enough income. Daddy had a solution for that, too.

"It's not hard to make a lot of money if you make that the most important thing in your life. Just apply yourself, work hard, join a country club, and socialize, socialize, socialize."

He did and it worked. By the time he was forty-two, Duane was a highly successful practitioner of adversary law with an impressive investment portfolio, a beautiful home in the best part of town, his and hers Mercedes in the garage, and two kids in an exclusive private school. He thought he should be happy, but he knew he wasn't. He felt exactly the way he did back in high school. In spite of all the socializing or maybe because of it, he didn't have a good friend and he wasn't having any fun. All he ever did was argue. If he wasn't in court arguing a case or at the office arguing with a client over the size of his fee or whether he was being aggressive enough in his attacks on the adversary, he was at home bickering with his wife who was angry because he never spent any time with her and the kids—which he didn't because his practice took it all up. His solutions had all come home to roost.

One day, sitting in the usual bumper-to-bumper traffic on the freeway, he turned on the car radio and heard Joseph Campbell talking about people who claw their way to the top of the ladder only to find it is up against the wrong wall. Duane felt as if he had just been hit with a baseball bat as the realization of how miserable his life was and how much pain he was in suddenly exploded in his head. When Professor Campbell went on to say that the surest way to keep this from happening is to follow your bliss, Duane hit on a solution for his predicament. He made up his mind to run away from home.

When he got to the office, he found a registered letter informing him that his wife was filing for divorce. Perfect. He wouldn't contest it. Some months later, his marriage was dissolved, his law practice disposed of, and

196

he was living in a cabin on the beach on the island of Maui, practicing hedonism instead of law. Hedonism is an ancient religion whose basic tenet is that single-minded pursuit of pleasure and avoidance of pain is the highest spiritual path that a human can aspire to. About a year and a half later, a phone call came into our center, which at that time was in Honolulu. The conversation went something like this.

"Transformational Learning Center, this is Susan."

"Hi, my name is Duane and I'm going to die."

(Long pause.) "We all have to die sometime, Duane. That's just how life is."

"My doctor says I should be dead in six months."

"Is that why you're going to die, because your doctor says you should?"

"That's what I wanted to talk to you guys about. I've been told you can help me explore viable alternatives. I'll be in town in about ten days to see that doctor. Maybe I can see you right after I see her."

"Sure."

When he came in for the appointment, Duane told us he had been diagnosed with leukemia and that the prognosis for the type he had was not very good. That's why he thought he was supposed to be dead in six months. "Today, she said I've been responding remarkably well to treatment and it looks like I might be going into remission. Now, she believes I have a fighting chance. She also said she believes I might profitably explore the possibility that my life-style had something to do with my getting sick. I've been turning that over

197

in my mind and it struck me that maybe what brought me down was an overdose of the good life. Two, actually. This second one damn near killed me."

One person's meat is another person's poison. So goes the old saying. That's how it was with the three personalities that add up to Duane. For one part of him, the masculine part, the good life was a life of money, power, prestige—and he had it all. For his shy, friendly, feminine personality and for his rambunctious inner child, it was a living hell. When the pain got to the point where he couldn't stand it anymore, Duane dumped the old life-style along with his inhibitions and put the kid in full charge. For this part of him, the good life was a life of uninterrupted drinking, smoking, and carousing. After eighteen months of this, he was eyeball to eyeball with a life-threatening disease. "I guess I kind of overcompensated," he said.

What he needed now was not another solution but a new direction. The best place to find that would be within himself, through a revelation. We told him daydreams are gold mines for revelations, and Duane agreed to go that route.

He pictured himself in conversation with Murtle, a sea turtle whose life he'd saved some months before. When he first met her, she was upside down on a rock and couldn't get back on her feet. Duane knew she would die for sure unless someone helped her out, so he flipped her over and pushed her back into the sea. Now, he pictured himself on the rock, chatting with her. He told her he was in trouble and asked if she could help him.

"Sure," she said. "I owe you one." He asked if she knew anything about his sickness, and the image of Murtle, who represented Duane's feminine personality, said she created it. "I'm doing for you exactly what you did for me. I bollixed your bloodstream to get you back into the mainstream."

That's when the revelation came. Duane realized how much time he had been spending flat on his back on the very same rock. Murtle said that unless he got off his butt and into productive, socially relevant activity, he would come to a bad end. This sickness was scary enough to pry him off the rock.

Duane said he felt he had just gotten great advice from a gifted psychic. Now, he didn't need a middle person to reveal his own truth to him. Following Murtle's advice, he sold his cabin on the beach and moved to California to start a new life.

About a year later, he sent us a letter saying he had finally gotten the three parts of himself to work as a team. He knew what he was doing must be right because his blood count was still normal after twelve months. His ego, the lawyer, was satisfied because he was back in practice. This time, instead of joining country clubs, socializing, and projecting images to insure success, what he did was take Murtle in as a full partner. His new practice focused on conflict resolution and catered to people who were interested in settling arguments peaceably. To make sure his inner child got its fair share of time, he was spending evenings and weekends volunteering at a community center, teaching little kids how to dance. On the advice of Murtle, with whom he still had regular chats, he contacted his ex-wife, and it was beginning to look like a reconciliation was a distinct possibility.

"I remember once hearing someone refer to cancer as 'the Great Liberator.' When I first heard that, it really bugged me because I had no idea how that could possibly be. Now, I can honestly say that getting leukemia might be the best thing that ever happened to me. It finally set me free."

For Jerry, the Great Liberator was a pain in the chest. Whereas Duane spent the first half of his adult life playing sickening social games. Jerry spent the first half of his playing Narcissus, the god who drowned in his own image. Jerry submerged himself in business. As long as he had the good sense to come up for air on weekends and holidays, all went well. But when he started finding more and more reasons for keeping his inner child submerged, it fought back.

A myth is a true story that never happened and is happening all the time. What Narcissus was supposed to have experienced physically, Jerry experienced psychologically. Whenever he looked into a mirror, he saw the image of a successful land developer. He liked what he saw and decided to totally identify with it. You could say that, like Narcissus, he fell in and got swallowed up by his own image. Jerry didn't actually drown. He just got hypnotized and forgot who he really was as well as what he started out to do.

As a young man, Jerry was an athlete and a party

animal. He loved sports, singing, dancing, and horsing around with friends. He also loved building things and was very good at it—good enough to become a professional builder. What he started out to do was earn enough to support himself while he spent most of his time doing what he felt like doing when he felt like doing it. His business grew by leaps and bounds and, before long, there was very little time for anything else. Then, he noticed that rich, successful builders seemed to get a lot more respect than happy-go-lucky party animals. This is when he fell in and allowed the land developer to swallow up the child, along with his creativity. Little by little, he got sucked deeper and deeper into the business, until he was totally immersed in it. What happened next was an early warning signal to let him know something was out of balance. At first, Jerry didn't recognize it as such and treated it as just another problem that needed to be solved.

One day, he woke up with a pain in his chest. It didn't last long, but it scared him so he went for a checkup. The doctor said his heart seemed fine at the moment, but his blood pressure was up so he would have to prescribe a drug to bring it down. The drug brought Jerry's pressure down and, along with it, his ability to function sexually. To Jerry's mind, this was a totally unacceptable trade-off. With his wife's encouragement and his doctor's approval, he dropped the drug and joined a meditation group because he read somewhere that meditating normalizes blood pressure with no side effects. He also got some biofeedback training and, after a month or two, was able to bring his pressure down without taking drugs. That was fine, but every once in a while, when he was really stressed out at work, he felt a vague sensation of tightness in his chest, and this worried him. When he came in for his first session, he told us why.

"I always thought I was immortal, that nothing could ever happen to me. But one day, this guy, a good five years younger than me, walked into the office and right in front of my eyes, keeled over with a heart attack. Then, as if I didn't have enough to worry about what with trying to keep my head above water in the middle of a recession, I start getting these stupid chest pains. Did you know that forty percent of first heart attacks are fatal? Since I read that, I have been starting each day believing it could be my last. My meditation teacher calls that enlightenment. She says if I could learn to live each day as if it really was my last, I wouldn't need the chest pains. In my younger days, I used to live as if this day is all there is, but I seem to have lost the knack. Thinking like that used to make me feel good. Now it just worries me. My doctor says worry and stress predispose people to heart attacks, and I've got plenty of both. He says I might think about a bypass operation to ease my mind. Preventive medicine with a radical surgical twist. A big part of me thinks I should just go ahead, replace the plumbing, and get it over with. Another part feels like there has got to be a better way. Then, there is this third part that is dead set against letting someone cut me open and muck around with my insides."

Jerry was very clear about the areas of disagreement

among the three parts of himself. The next step was creating a character to represent each point of view and imagine a conference in which they negotiate a win-win-win resolution to his inner conflict. To play the part of the hard driving, get-the-job-done land developer, Jerry decided to use a movie actor—John Wayne. Then, he closed his eyes for a few minutes to see what kind of childlike image might come to mind. He remembered a little girl, about five, he had seen in a playground, taking her first ride down a slide. He said the expression on her face was priceless. "Scared, excited, and amazed all at the same time. I remember feeling exactly like that when I was a kid," he went on. "Back in the days when I knew I was immortal. I remember her name was Betsy."

Having personified his masculine aspect and his inner child, he needed to create one more character to portray his feminine personality. He couldn't think of anyone, and no image came to mind so he tried a different tack. We asked him to list the most prominent characteristics of a few important women in his life. He said those would be his wife, his secretary, and his meditation teacher, in that order. He described his wife as "loving, creative, and a natural born comic." He saw his secretary as "capable, efficient, and a closet environmentalist with liberal leanings." His meditation teacher was "a wise old woman with a New York accent and a sharp tongue."

"Can you think of an actress who might play the part of a woman with those characteristics?" Susan asked.

"Sure," he said. "Barbra Streisand." Jerry looked at her image with his mind's eye and during his next out breath thought the words, "What shall I call you?" As he was breathing in, the name "Sophia" popped into his mind. "I wonder where that came from," he said. "I don't know anyone named Sophia." Then he chuckled. "I guess I do now."

Jerry was here at the Oregon coast on vacation. When you vacate, you clear out of someplace and leave it behind. The way you did when you left your momma's womb. Jerry's current vacation from his habitual lifestyle was temporary—eight days. The idea was to see if, while he was here, he could find a way of living that would allow him to be symptom free. The technique we were teaching him at TLC uses the symptom as a stepping-stone to that new way of life. It's based on the theory that symptoms and other crises are, like black holes in space, gateways to other universes.

Jerry began the process of balancing his three personalities by picturing himself and his allies seated around a poolside table at a posh resort. Step 1 was to describe the thing that was bothering him most in the simplest possible terms so little Betsy would understand what he was talking about. Since a picture is worth a thousand words, Jerry began by converting his symptom into a visual image. He said it felt as if there was a big balloon in his chest that someone kept blowing up. "It hurts, and I'm scared it might burst and then I'll be dead."

Step 2 involves watching for thoughts to come to mind on the in breath. Each thought is arbitrarily assigned to one of the allies. You make believe one of them said it. As he was breathing in, Jerry found himself thinking, "Why am I sitting around here playing stupid mind games when I should be in the hospital getting my coronary arteries reamed out?"

Jerry decided that had to be John. The next thought that popped into his mind made him laugh. It was what his meditation teacher would have said in response to that remark.

"So, tell me, Mr. Big Shot, if you're so smart, how come you're sick? For your information," she continued, "what we have here is an open-and-shut case of heartache, for which, as everyone knows, there is no such thing as a surgical cure."

Obviously, that was Sophia. Jerry sensed that although she and John did not see eye to eye on what to do about it, neither was responsible for the balloon in his chest. Susan suggested he ask Betsy if she knew who was. Jerry imagined Betsy looking down at her shoes, admitting it was her balloon and that she was the one blowing it up. He asked her why, and she said to make him pay attention to her because there was something important she needed to tell him.

Daydreams, once we get into them, take on a life of their own. As they spontaneously unfold, they generate insights and reveal things about ourselves we could never figure out because they are inaccessible to the rational mind. When Jerry told Betsy she now had his full attention and he was ready to hear what she wanted to tell him, he got one of those insights.

"It's all his fault," she said, pointing a finger at John. "He never lets me out to play anymore, so, when I get bored, I play with my balloon. Every time I blow it up, he gets scared and acts funny. I like that."

For the first time ever, it dawned on Jerry that there might be a connection between his aching heart and his pleasure-deficient life-style. He said he had been getting that message from his wife for years, but until now, he never heard it. "She keeps telling me I've turned into a workaholic and I'm no fun anymore. I guess I got so wrapped up in my work I forgot there are other things just as important."

Incorporating this insight into his daydream, Jerry decided that by completely identifying with John, he had neglected Sophia and Betsy. Tightness in the chest was their way of communicating this to him and of letting him know they were demanding equal time. Since right now is the only time there is, we suggested Jerry might think about doing something that very day to put some balance back into his life. Since he couldn't figure out what to do, he agreed it might be a good idea to ask Betsy what he could do for her, in return for which she would refrain from blowing up her balloon for the rest of the day. The idea being that the only day you can be well is today, and, if you can string enough well days together, back to back, what you have is a cure.

Jerry was really surprised when Betsy said what she wanted to do was build a sand castle. John balked. The notion that he, a grown man, was now supposed to go play in the sand just because an imaginary five-year-old said he should struck him as stupid and embarrassing. Betsy started crying and fingering her balloon. Jerry felt a twinge of tightness in his chest and wondered what to do next.

When two of our selves come into conflict like this, the third (the neutral one) becomes a mediator. At first, Sophia sided with Betsy. She also took the opportunity to get a few licks of her own in.

"What would be stupid, Mr. Land Baron," she said, "would be to fall on the floor with a heart attack. Which is what could happen if you don't wise up and get real here, pretty soon. What would be embarrassing would be to leave as a memorial a bunch of ticky-tacky developments and ugly shopping malls where natural beauty used to be. You are no Frank Lloyd Wright, you know. Compared to some of that stuff you built after I told you how ugly it was, a nice little sand castle would be a work of art."

This kind of talk, coming from Sophia, didn't surprise Jerry. He had a hunch his secretary felt like this, and he knew his wife did because she told him so. Two-thirds of him wanted to build a sand castle. One-third was appalled. What this added up to was tightness in his chest.

If you change one factor in an equation, you change the result. Dr. Oyle said John might change his mind and agree to go along with the other two if there was a cookie in it for him—relief of the chest discomfort, for instance. Sophia said if it would make it easier for him, they could build the sand castle on a deserted stretch of beach near the condo Jerry had rented for the week so no one would see and there would be nothing to be embarrassed about. John reluctantly agreed. Betsy smiled, put down her balloon, and, as she did, Jerry felt the tension in his chest relax.

"That is amazing," he said. "Do you think it might work for insomnia, too?"

Jerry guessed he wasn't sleeping because he, John, couldn't or wouldn't stop worrying about his business and about his health. Now that he had seen how negotiating with Betsy could make his chest stop aching, he was more confident. But how could he be sure it wasn't just a coincidence? And if it wasn't, the implication that she had so much power over his physical body was a situation he didn't relish thinking about. At this point, something his meditation teacher was always telling him popped into Jerry's mind. He imagined Sophia saying it to John.

"You know what your trouble is? You think too much. When you don't think, you can't worry. This, my friend, is a well-known fact. So stop thinking and you won't worry. If you don't worry, you'll feel peaceful. If you feel peaceful, you'll sleep—there is nothing to it."

We asked Jerry how lack of sleep was affecting his life. He said that after being up all night he would come into work grumpy and irritable. Then, he would spend his workday snapping at people and biting their heads off. Employees, suppliers, even investors. In addition, he was making business decisions that wound up costing him piles of money. When he got home, he would argue with his wife and stay awake all night worrying about everything that had happened because he hadn't slept the night before. If he tried drinking himself into oblivion and/or taking sleeping pills, he woke up with a horrendous hangover, which put him out of commission for the whole day. "It's not a pretty picture," he said.

Susan wondered if Sophia might be disturbing Jerry's sleep to attract his attention. He imagined himself asking her. Sophia said the insomnia was a wonderful way to do with his business what he was doing with her creative talents. "Nice you noticed," she said.

"See if you can strike another deal," said Susan. "Ask what you can do for her today in return for which she'll let you sleep tonight. Keep your end of the bargain, and watch what happens."

Sophia said he could start by taking his watch off, putting it in his pocket, and promising not to look at it for the rest of the day. Then she added, "Better you should put a piece of masking tape over the face so you can't see it." Jerry said the thought of not being able to know what time it was made him nervous. We talked about how the sensation he was interpreting as nervousness was a flow of free energy that could just as easily be experienced as exhilaration. We gave him some masking tape, and he did what Sophia asked him to do. Sure enough, as soon as he put the taped watch into his pocket, what started out as a twinge of anxiety turned into a sense of freedom. This felt so good, he decided he would leave his watch with us for the rest of the day.

This done, Sophia said he should take a nice, long walk on the beach, build a sand castle, and, when it was finished, just sit there and watch the sun go down.

Jerry was curious to see if this stuff would really work, so he followed Sophia's instructions to the letter.

He found a deserted stretch of beach and got so involved in building an elaborate sand castle that he lost track of time. Then, he noticed a glorious sunset was well underway, so he just sat and watched it. As the afterglow faded and stars appeared, he realized he was feeling better than he had since since God knows when. On a scale of one to ten, he was a solid ten. Sitting there, hypnotized by the sound of breaking waves, the first thought he had had all afternoon crossed his mind.

"So, Mr. Master Builder, now you know what life is like when you let the rest of us get into the act and share some of your precious time."

Jerry laughed out loud, walked back to town for Betsy, and went to see a movie, which turned out to be about a man having to share his body with the spirit of a woman. That night, he slept like a log and, in the morning, woke up feeling fit as a fiddle.

John was impressed—so much so that he agreed to let the other two do whatever they felt like doing whenever they felt like doing it, but only for that week. In return, Sophia and Betsy promised to let Jerry sleep all night and be pain free all day, but only for that week.

During our daily sessions, Jerry asked each of his allies what they felt like doing that day. Then, he did it. As a result, he went back to living the life he had lived before he fell in and got swallowed up by the goal-obsessed businessman in him. This included walking on the beach, fishing, swimming, dancing, going to parties, clowning around, and generally enjoying himself. By the end of the sixth day, he was still symptom free and feeling twenty years younger.

On day seven of his personal program at TLC, Jerry found himself face-to-face with a universal principle. Every action has an equal and opposite reaction. He totally fell apart as a prelude to reintegration on a higher level. At the time, he wasn't aware of this. All he knew was that he was going through some kind of crisis, and it didn't feel very good. He told us that after a good night's sleep, he woke up to the realization that his vacation was almost over. That sent him into what he called "a blue funk." As he settled in for our next to last session, he was feeling agitated, angry, and depressed. He said his chest was tight and the back of his neck felt like someone had it clamped in a vise.

When dealing with unpleasant emotions and/or physical symptoms, a good first step is to separate yourself from them by projecting them on to one or more imaginary characters in a daydream. Jerry accomplished this by having his allies act out a little skit that gave us a bird's eye view of what was going on within him right then. After taking several slow, deep breaths, during which he silently repeated the phrases, "I am relaxed, I am peaceful, I am tranquility," he was calm enough to picture his allies at the poolside table.

"Just watch them the way you would watch a TV

show," Dr. Oyle said. "Watching animates them. Tell us what you see them doing next."

After a moment of silence, Jerry chuckled. "This is really funny," he said. "John is halfway out of his chair, hell-bent to get back home and into harness as soon as possible. Sophia has hold of him by the scruff of the neck and is yanking him back, yelling, 'I'm mad as hell, and I'm not going to take it anymore.' Betsy is howling and puffing into her blue balloon."

We asked him to expand this opening scene into a daydream. "Use your own thoughts, emotions, and recent events in your life as raw material. See if you can write it as a situation comedy that has no bad guys and a happy ending. In that context, what do you imagine might happen next?"

Then, like any other creative process, Jerry's daydream took on a life of its own. He just watched it unfold as the three of us sat around, like writers at a story conference, guiding it. Actually, Jerry was the writer. Susan and Dr. Oyle asked questions, so they could follow the story, and offered occasional suggestions for Jerry's consideration. We asked him why he thought Betsy was yowling, and he said he guessed it was because she didn't want to leave the resort. Since they all lived within Jerry, she and Sophia would be dragged along if John got his way. Betsy said she was puffing on the balloon to see if she could bust it and if that would make John fall down and go boom just like the funny man in the office did. Jerry remembered the investor with the heart attack and felt a twinge of fear, which he projected onto

John. He imagined John turning pale and slumped back into his chair.

"He's not dead," Jerry assured us, "just scared. If he were speaking for the rational part of me, which I guess he is, he would say that lying around at the seashore and living like a hippie is fine for a week or so, but in the real world it doesn't put bread on the table. I've got responsibilities and some pretty heavy fixed expenses which, as much as I love to do it, I'll never meet by building sand castles."

Susan wondered what Sophia's response to that might be, and Jerry said that Sophia answered, "If Betsy busts your balloon, Mr. Financial Wizard, maybe you'll meet your responsibilities from a plot in a cemetery. You could take care of them during your coffee breaks from pushing up daisies. At least that way, you'll get to sleep. Even if you go in for an operation to have Betsy's balloon removed, you'll still have to worry about how you are going to get some sleep. Unless you figure out a way to solve that problem, which you have already found out you can't, you know your business is going down the tubes, which it already did."

We asked Jerry what she meant by this, and he said it must have been a reference to one of his land development schemes that backfired. Using other people's money, he recently started building a shopping mall on the outskirts of a thriving community. Before it was finished, a large military facility, the town's biggest employer, was shut down. The community's economy went belly-up, and Jerry's land development project went down the drain, taking a good deal of investors' money with it.

Having lost other people's money was upsetting to Sophia, but it didn't seem to bother John. He said that everyone knows that any investment carries an element of risk. Besides, his attorneys had assured him that, legally, he was in the clear. All he wanted to do now was to get back to the office so he could round up some new investors to start another project in a different area. When we asked him how he imagined Sophia might feel about this, the conflict festering within Jerry exploded like a ripe abscess. Sophia was furious.

"So, Mr. Fly by Night," he imagined her saying to John, "you'll just step over the corpses and find yourself another beautiful piece of land to rape and turn into ticky-tacky disgustingness. Keep it up, and you'll wind up like that poor devil who keeled over in your office after he found out you had buried his life savings under a pile of concrete."

With that, Jerry had a revelation. In a flash of insight, he clearly saw how intensely two-thirds of him hated the business and how terrified another part of him, John, was of giving it up. Susan wanted to know what he was so scared of.

"Death, I guess," Jerry said. "But something scares him or me even more. Last year, I was on a business trip to Tokyo, and the airline sent my bags to the wrong city. An agent tracked them down and told me they would be on a carousel at the Tokyo airport in a little less than four hours. He even showed me which one. It was early in the day, so I decided to take a bus into town and do a little sight-seeing. After a couple of hours wandering around, I had no idea of where I was or how to get back to the airport, so I figured I had better take a taxi. When I reached for my billfold to see if I had enough yen, it was gone. There I was, lost and alone in a foreign country with no passport and no money. Nothing but the clothes on my back. The jolt of panic I felt then is exactly how I feel now whenever I think of my business going under."

"The minute you lost your billfold," said Susan, "you were in that predicament. How were you feeling between the time it actually disappeared and the minute you noticed it was gone?"

"Having a wonderful time," Jerry said. "Ignorance is bliss, I guess."

"So it wasn't the situation you were in that made you panic," Susan said. "It was your perception of it."

Doctor Oyle pointed out that as a newborn, Jerry had been in an even worse predicament. "Not only were you without money or a passport, you were also naked, helpless, and blind. How did you cope with it?"

"At first," said Jerry, confusing his adult predicament with the one his child self had successfully navigated, "I just stood there with sweaty palms, running a whole bunch of disaster scenarios through my head. That would have been John. Then, I remembered something my meditation teacher told us. Putting it in terms of the game we are playing here, I would say Sophia reminded me that everything anyone ever needs is always within thirty feet of them. So I looked around and sure enough, about ten feet from where I was standing, I saw an English couple window-shopping. They drove me to the American Embassy, and the folks there helped me get everything squared away."

"So Sophia got you through that one," Doctor Oyle said. "What about the bloody mess you were in right after you got born? You didn't think your way out of that, either. You relied on your instinctive self, Betsy, and did whatever you felt like doing whenever you felt like doing it. When you felt hungry, you cried. When you were nursed, you suckled. When you felt full, you slept. Whenever you felt the urge, you relieved yourself. Before you knew it, you were up and walking on your own. Is there any reason to believe the same strategy won't get you through this crisis?"

"You're telling me," Jerry said, "that if I go home and keep on living like I've been living here, doing what a couple of figments of my own imagination tell me to do, my problems will solve themselves? That would require a leap of faith I don't think I'm capable of."

"The leap," said Susan, "would be off a sinking ship. Besides, what other choice do you have? You can go back home and do some more of what didn't work before and hope the strategy that created chest pains, insomnia, and a floundering business last time will bring health, happiness, and success if you give it one more chance. What kind of sense does that make?"

Jerry knew she was right. What with the recession, a credit crunch because banks were up to their ears in bad real estate loans, and an increasingly militant environmental movement, the land development business was not what it used to be. He realized he was at the end of a rope that was slipping through his fingers. Hanging on with all his might raised his blood pressure and made his chest hurt. The thought of letting go terrified him. But, now, he was looking at the real possibility that he might kill himself trying to earn a living. This was so because for John, Jerry's masculine personality, fear of failure was stronger than fear of death. "I'd rather die than quit," was how he put it. Jerry's inner child, represented by Betsy, seemed more than willing to accommodate him.

Sophia said he didn't have to do either right away. She reminded him that the doctor had asked him to come back in three months for a follow-up checkup and suggested that he could use that block of time to extend this vacation into a mini-sabbatical and see if things would work themselves out the way they did in Tokyo. Jerry had to admit that, over the past few days, living as he had, he was sleeping well and feeling no pain. John said that taking a break to see if he could maintain his state of well-being and avoid major surgery made sense. He thought three months was a bit much but said he could afford it if he just lived at home. When he realized that he might even be able to collect on his income protection insurance policy, he decided he would go along with the scheme. Betsy and Sophia were delighted, and everyone agreed this was a giant step toward a happy ending for Jerry's daydream.

There was one problem. John's ingrained habit of worrying and churning out endless streams of disaster scenarios involving poverty, starvation, and homelessness was an ongoing source of stress. "Meditating shuts him up and that feels good," Jerry said. "But I can't spend all my time contemplating my navel just to keep him off my back. He isn't really a bad guy, you know. It's just that he thinks survival depends on figuring things out, taking the bull by the horns, and making the world do what he thinks it should be doing. He just figured out that's impossible, so he is scared because he doesn't know what else to do."

"He could transform," Susan said.

To us, Jerry's remarks indicated a quantum leap in consciousness on his part. Like someone coming out of a hypnotic trance, he had disentangled himself from and ceased to identify with his ego, the businessman. He realized it was one way he could be and not who he really was. Since John Wayne had taken Jerry as far as he could go, it was obviously time for Jerry to find a new way of being, a new male ally.

So, back at the imaginary resort, Jerry asked his allies what they thought he needed to do in time and space, that very day, to accomplish this. Betsy, the child and the oldest and wisest of the three, said she felt like going for a swim and building another sand castle on the beach. Jerry laughed and promised to do this right after the session was over. At the time, he had no idea how prophetic her suggestion was.

"While you're there," Sophia said, "you should dig a nice

deep hole in the sand and burn those business cards you brought along in case someone might ask you who you were, since that isn't who you are anymore. Burying them would show you really mean business. Besides, you have plenty more back home, so what is the big deal?"

Jerry was surprised at how much resistance he had to doing this. He said he felt like he was being asked to murder a part of himself. Doctor Oyle told him not to worry because those cards only represented his ego, the businessman. As such it couldn't be murdered, only transformed. "The way Superman, the man of steel who can leap tall buildings with a single bound, ducks into a telephone booth and comes out Clark Kent, a mild-mannered reporter."

John said transformation was no problem. If changing form was all it would take to make everyone happy, they could sure count on him. Then, he tipped his hat, strolled over to a poolside cabana, disappeared inside, and closed the door behind him. Seconds later, the door opened again, and a different movie actor who was soft-spoken and a lot less macho, Alan Alda, came out. He asked them all to call him Paul. After giving Sophia a big hug, Paul scooped Betsy up into his arms, parked himself in John's chair with her in his lap, looked at Jerry and said, "How may I serve you?"

With that, Jerry remembered why he went into business in the first place — so he could earn enough money to keep a roof over his head, food on the table, and clothes on his back while spending the bulk of his time building beautiful things, having fun, and generally enjoying life. But he forgot what he started out to do, and before long, the tail was wagging the dog. Instead of collecting money as a means to an end, he got into it full-time. Like the dog in Aesop's fable, he dropped the enjoyable life-style he had in the early days and totally immersed himself in business so he could make piles of money to buy lots of things supposedly to have an even more enjoyable life-style. All he got for his trouble were chest pains and sleepless nights.

Now, thanks to a downturn in the economy, he had a chance to begin again and get it right. So, in answer to Paul's question, Jerry said. "You can help me figure out a way to earn a living without getting sick."

"The right livelihood isn't something you can figure out. John tried and look how it turned out," said Paul. "It might make more sense to let Betsy and Sophia guide you to it. They already told you what they want you to do today."

"It looks as if I'm back to the leap of faith off a sinking ship," Jerry said. "It seems like there's no way to avoid it. Sure would be nice to have a life preserver."

"Keep an open mind," Susan said. "Besides, we are only talking about today. You got through a whole day in Tokyo without possessions, identification, or money. What would keep you from getting through a whole day here without business cards?"

"Fear, I guess," said Jerry, "Like in this dream I had when I spent the whole night running away from someone or something that was chasing me. I have no idea who or what it was. I just know it scared the hell out of me. What do you suppose it means?"

"Imagine each dream figure is an aspect of yourself, one of your allies," Doctor Oyle advised. "Then, dream up a happy ending right now. The meaning will come to you."

Jerry decided the one running scared was John. He imagined his former ally ducking into a phone booth and coming out Paul. Paul, who was curious rather than fearful, calmly leaned against the phone booth and waited for his pursuer to catch up to him so he could see who it was. According to the rules, it had to be one of Jerry's allies, and it turned out to be Betsy. She said she'd been running after John because she wanted to get him to play with her. She was glad to see he had been turned into Paul because it looked as if now he'd be a lot more fun. Paul picked Betsy up and, in a flash, they were all back at the poolside table with her in his lap, celebrating their new relationship. And that was the happy ending to Jerry's daydream.

Jerry was amazed at how much better he felt about everything. He said the dream made him realize that all those years in the construction business had turned John into a firm believer in Murphy's law. Faced with anything new or unfamiliar, he always presumed the worst. Paul apparently presumed the best.

Susan wondered whether John had any religious belief. Jerry said he believed he owed his existence to a power greater than himself and that, after creating him, he, she or it dropped him into this world and left him to make it on his own. When Susan asked how Paul's belief differed from John's, Jerry said he wasn't sure, but he would check inside and see. He closed his eyes, and a radio interview he had heard that very morning came to mind.

"This doctor was talking about how come some people get well even though they are not supposed to. You know, miracle cures and stuff like that. He said he believes there is some inherent pattern and rightness and wholeness to the universe that has a strong tendency to turn chaos into order and sickness into health. All we have to do, according to him, is get out of the way. Like when you've tried everything and nothing works and you give up and accept your fate. Business-wise, that's where I'm at, so I guess there is hope for me."

"Anyhow," Jerry continued, "this is what Paul believes. It's the flip side of Murphy's law, which says if something can possibly go wrong it probably will. I don't have to do anything. It just happens on its own. The laws of physics say that every action has an equal and opposite reaction. There is nothing I have to do to make that happen, either. All I can do is inhibit it by getting in the way. So, when everything seems to have gone wrong, if I stay out of the way, anything that can possibly go right, probably will. Sounds good to me. I'm willing to give it a try, except I don't know how to get out of the way."

"That happened when you transformed John," Doctor Oyle said. "He was programmed to believe that making money was more important than feeling good and having fun, which is putting the cart before the horse.

Now that he is gone, maybe things will turn around the way Paul says they will."

Then, the session ended with talk about holographic theory, the Gaia hypothesis, and how a change of belief can change your life. Jerry said he guessed it was time for him to be off to do his homework. "Go for a swim and burn my business cards. I'm still a little nervous about that second chore, but Sophia's telling me to be brave and expect a miracle. Paul says that tearing them up and throwing them into the trash will work just as well, but Betsy says burning them seems like more fun, so that's what I'll do."

At the beach, Jerry burned the cards, buried the ashes, and plunged into the sea. Initiation by fire and water. Coming out, he felt like a different person. No more land developer. So who was he, and what was he supposed to do now?

Paul thought he should sit quietly and wait for instructions. He did, and they came quickly. Betsy told him to build another sand castle, a big one. "And a gorgeous one," Sophia said. Since he had nothing better to do, Jerry got totally involved in building an elaborate sand castle, immersing himself as completely in this project as he had in John's construction business. The next thing he knew, the sun was going down and a nice looking older couple was admiring his handiwork. In the glowing light of the sunset, it was truly beautiful. The wife wondered whether he was a sculptor. Jerry was surprised to hear himself tell her he was a retired builder. That must have been Paul.

"I'm recently retired myself," said the husband. "How long has it been for you?"

"Since about eleven this morning," Jerry said.

As they chatted, Jerry learned that they'd just bought some property on which they were planning to build a new home for themselves. They had no idea how to go about it and wondered whether Jerry would be willing to give them some pointers. "Naturally," the husband said, "we'd be willing to pay for your time and expertise." And that was how Jerry got started on his new career.

The wife noticed an incoming tide lapping at the foundations of Jerry's castle. "Isn't that a pity," she said, "in a couple of hours it will be gone without a trace."

"That is okay," Jerry said, "it has already served its purpose. Besides, there are zillions more where that one came from."

MORAL: THE UNIVERSE KNOWS WHAT IT IS DOING AND IS RIGGED IN YOUR FAVOR.

13

Your Turn, Dear Reader

One who knows others is wise.
One who knows oneself is enlightened.
LAO-TZU

Want to learn to play the game of life better? To be more flexible and spontaneous? To adapt to the life from which the soul can most benefit?

Throughout this book, you've read the stories of people who explored their inner worlds and received valuable information. Now, it's your turn to learn who your own inner allies are. They've been waiting to meet with you and give you answers to whatever questions are uppermost in your mind right now.

Pick a time in the next day or two when you can be alone, undisturbed, and quiet for an hour. If you enjoy the outdoors, that's a good place to be. If you have a favorite place at home that's quiet and restful, stay there, and put on some soft music if you feel like it.

Read through the following exercise a couple of times, then set the book aside and allow yourself to relax and enjoy the show! You can proceed slowly by reading a section at a time, then put the book down and do what you've just read.

Begin by sitting comfortably. Focus on your breathing. Take deep, slow, even breaths. Watch yourself breathe. Closing your eyes may help you to center your attention on just breathing. As it becomes comfortable for you, slow your breathing down gradually.

Now that your breathing has a steady, slow rhythm, on your next in breath think to yourself the words *I am*. Then, as you breathe out, think to yourself the word *relaxed*. Stretch these words the entire length of each breath. Repeat "I am" each time you breathe in and "relaxed" each time you breathe out.

If you'd prefer a different word than *relaxed*, try *peaceful, calm, tranquil,* or *serene*. Find the one that works best for you, or use a couple of them alternatively. Play with them a little to see what feels good and holds your attention. Remember, the point is to stay focused on your breathing.

If you haven't already, let your eyes close as you continue to take deep, slow, even breaths. Begin to imagine that, as you breathe in, a wave of soothing energy flows up the front of your body to the top of your head. As you breathe out, it slides down your back, down the backs of your legs, and out the bottoms of your heels into the ground. As you practice this, imagine that you can use this energy during each breath to swirl around any area of discomfort, pain, or tension in your body. See the energy soothing and relaxing the area as you direct it with each breath.

With a little practice at circulating this soothing energy, some people see it as a white, pink, or golden light. Others feel it as a warmth or tingling.

Allow yourself to do just the breathing and energy circulation until you feel nice and relaxed. A state of peaceful alertness is the ideal. For your first time through this, do as much as feels right for you and then move onto the next step.

As you continue breathing deeply and slowly, imagine a beautiful natural place. It can be a mountain meadow, a tropical paradise, a cozy campground. Select a place you've actually been or make one up right now that has the elements of natural beauty you like best. Just be sure it's a wonderful place to rest and relax, so that it feels good just to be there.

Now, picture yourself strolling through this safe, quiet scene. Enjoy the feel of the ground or grass or sand under your feet. As you walk, you begin to smell the smells and hear the sounds that are there naturally. Become aware of all the colors that surround you.

As you are exploring your beautiful favorite place, look around and select a comfortable place to sit down—a chaise lounge, a large pillow against the trunk of a tree, even a recliner, if you like. Because this is your imaginary play, you can make whatever you want to sit on appear, right where you want it, so treat yourself well.

Seat yourself and continue to focus on your breathing as you relax after your walk. Look around again and begin to experience more of the details of your surroundings—a breeze in the trees, the smell of flowers, or birds gliding by overhead.

As you are enjoying just being there, you become aware of some friendly presence attracting your attention. It might be an animal, a human, a celestial body, an object . . . anything. Once you've noticed this new friend, greet it (with a handshake, a smile, a hug, or a simple "hello") and make friends with it. If it's an animal, feed it (remember, in this play you can create whatever you wish as you go along, so creating the appropriate food is as easy as deciding what it is and then picturing it in your hand). If it's a human, treat her or him as you would a special guest in your home. If your new friend is inanimate—a rock or a tree or a star—treat it like a real being, because it is. The ally you've just met is ready, willing, and able to serve you and answer your questions, so treat this new friend accordingly.

First, let's find out what your new friend's name is. As you breathe out, look at your ally and think the words "What shall I call you?" As you breathe in, leave your mind blank, and a name will come to you. Staying relaxed and breathing deeply, allow this type of communication to happen easily. Take the first name that comes and let it be okay with you.

Keep in mind that this is a simple fantasy play that you are making up as you go along. You are the producer and the director. So as you watch the images as well as being a player in the scene, remember that you are creating the show. That's the basic paradoxical truth here.

Therefore, if you're sitting and breathing, yet no ally appears and nothing that is there naturally calls your attention, you can select a favorite public figure, fictional character, or cartoon image, to be your ally. Put this ally in your beautiful place with you. It's as easy as that.

Now, you and your first ally can sit down together for a good talk. Create a new chair or whatever your ally would prefer to settle on to be comfortable. Invite her or him to join you in your special seating area in your beautiful place.

Spend a minute selecting our first question as you continue to focus on your breathing—deep, slow, and even. Choose the issue or relationship or symptom that is uppermost in your mind today. Think of what you would want to ask about it if you were to have a chance to consult with a wise and all-knowing entity, or had access to the most knowledgeable computer on earth. Phrase your question clearly and briefly, such as, "Why am I _____?" or "What should I do about _____?" or "What's _____ teaching me?"

Focus again on taking deep, slow breaths. Remember clearly your beautiful favorite place and your ally sitting with you, ready to talk. Call your ally by name. Reach out and touch or hold your ally. As you breathe out, think your question. Let your mind stay blank as you breathe in (your *in*-spirational breath) and your ally's answer will come to you. The answer may be in words, or your ally may act it out, so listen and watch. Allies always answer, but it may take a little time for you to get used to receiving answers from within yourself. The more you practice, the easier it gets.

If the answer you get is not clear to you, tell your ally on your next out breath that you don't understand and need a clearer answer. Or, ask another question to get more information. Keep talking with your ally until you get a clear answer, some sense of enlightenment, or a new perspective on the situation.

Then, thank your ally for the guidance. If you'd like, agree to meet with this new friend once (or twice or three times) each day to get more assistance and talk about other concerns as they come up for you. It's best to agree to meet during your quiet times, so you can give your full attention to this and have a little time to digest the valuable information you will be receiving. Some days you'll have a lot of questions, and other days you may just do some deep breathing, take a minute to thank your ally for always being there for you, and do a little celebration with your ally because everything is going so well.

It's also a good idea to meet with your ally when something surprises or worries you during the day. Just stop and take a few deep breaths. Then imagine your favorite place, call your ally by name, and ask what the purpose of the event or feeling is. Ask what its message is for you. Then let your ally guide you out of the uncomfortable feeling and back to peacefulness. It's much easier than trying to think your way out.

Now that you've begun to see the value of talking with an inner ally, let's go on to the next step—meeting your other two allies. Follow the same steps you did to meet the first one. Look around till the next one attracts your attention. Make friends, and have the second ally settle in at your special meeting area. Ask questions to get guidance about whatever is uppermost in your mind. Thank the ally and agree to meet regularly. Do the same to meet your third ally.

When your family of allies is complete, you will have

created one child, one female, and one male. They may be quite different from one another in form. The child may be a porpoise, the female a squirrel, and the male a gladiator. Accept their forms as you first see them, for now. The form can be part of the message they are giving you.

Once you have talked with each of the three until you are satisfied that you understand their answers, gather them all close to you, because you will now be asking them for the most important information they have to give you. Ask each of them individually, "What shall I do today?" Listen carefully to the answer. Have a pen and paper handy so you can write down what they say.

As each ally answers, consider whether it is possible for you to do what the ally is requesting. If the ally wants lunch on the moon, you may have to negotiate by offering an approximate alternative. Be sure the ally is genuinely pleased with the change you suggest. Otherwise, ask what the ally's second choice is for today.

If the ally just wants to walk barefoot in the park, and the only real reason not to is that you have a full schedule of people to see, things to do, and places to go, stop and consider the ally's desire seriously. It may be exactly what you most need today to add a little balance to your goal-directed life.

Once you have clear guidance from all three allies, promise them you will carry out their instructions TODAY. The difference they can make in your sense of well-being can't be described—it can only be experienced.

You have quite a treat in store for you each day you follow your allies' advice. And, what's more, the effect is cumulative. So begin as soon as possible. Enjoying today each day can become a wonderful habit.

So, once again, thank each of your allies for their wisdom, guidance, and friendship. Then, have a celebration in which all four of you join together to express your joy and love. It could be a dance, a swim, a glass of champagne, or a formal ceremony. Let them show you the celebration in your imagery, and then you join in so that all four of you are sharing the feeling of the celebration. Let the event reach its natural, harmonious conclusion.

Then, with your three best friends, your allies, all settled into your beautiful, favorite place, gradually come back into the time-space world. Allow your eyes to open as you reenter the peace and quiet of your other favorite place. Remember the assignments they gave you for today. They are your teachers, and they are guiding you unerringly to a better life.

Now, a few points of note for you, dear reader, as you digest this experience. If you are among those who have *believed* that you are unable to visualize, please know that if you can describe the difference between your car key and your house key, or your face and that of your mother, you are already visualizing. We all visualize all the time. It's just that, because it's such a simple, natural ability, we don't realize we're doing it. So allow this inner movie-making mechanism to serve you as you produce and direct the show. Just remember that each of your actors has a mind of its own.

It's important to be aware of the interactions among your three allies. By nature, their viewpoints are each quite different. Therefore, disagreements are the norm. The key to resolving these is to have the allies with opposite opinions negotiate to the point of consensus, where they both win. This may take a little practice, but the rewards are well worth it—a sense of inner peace instead of inner turmoil. In any conflict, the third ally is the neutral party, and, because of this detached perspective, can offer advice on how the two who are at odds can reach consensus.

Another point of interest is that the first part of this procedure, the deep breathing and energy circulation, can be used during the resolving of inner conflicts between the allies and also those interpersonal conflicts you encounter during your day-to-day life. When stress and/or fatigue are inhibiting progress, take a few deep breaths, feel your soothing energy swirling within you, relaxing and tranquilizing, and stroll through your favorite beautiful place for a moment or two. That refreshing change in focus will give you a new perspective on whatever needs resolving. Once you have practiced this a few times, it's quite easy to do, even with your eyes open, anywhere you are. Try it the next time you are late for an appointment or stuck in traffic or hear someone say something you don't like.

As you prepare to meet your allies, after reading this chapter through a couple of times, there are ways to make it easier and more fun. You may wish to make an audio cassette tape of the instructions so you can sit with your eyes closed throughout the experience. Be sure to leave long pauses where needed. Then, sit back and watch the show while you really listen to and feel the answers.

It works equally well to have a close friend read this exercise to you. An added bonus to this variation is that you get to share the answers right away with someone who will encourage you to remember them, take them to heart, and remodel your day accordingly.

We wish you pleasant, productive daydreams!

14

Common Sense

Therefore I say unto you,
all things for which you pray and ask,
believe that you have received them,
they shall be granted to you.
MARK 11:24

Having met your allies, it is normal now to have at least as many questions as you have answers. This simply indicates that the process has begun. You have activated or at least become aware of a perpetually active inquisitiveness within yourself.

You will progress from this point at whatever speed to whatever level of proficiency you choose. Please be aware, though, that it is easier to float down the river than try to swim upstream to yesterday's status quo.

The natural balancing process you've begun to learn about in this book has always been and will always be an integral part of you. Getting to know the inner you better makes life easier. Ignoring your inner world creates backlogs of unresolved conflicts, negative emotions, and such confusion that simple, joyful living is difficult at best.

As encouragement to you on this inner quest, we present here some basic rules for getting the most out of what appears to be going on "out there."

Rules of the Game

1. Everyone you see has something to teach you.
2. Any problem you see someone dealing with, especially if you feel a charge of energy (either a positive or negative emotion), can be a clue to your own unfoldment.
3. Therefore, please listen carefully to any advice you give to them because that is the best advice for *you* because *you* came up with it.
4. Don't be a victim of your relationships, your body, or your life. You put yourself in these situations to learn your own magnificent, limitless potential to evolve, strengthen yourself, and become a more capable, wonderful human being.
5. THE ANSWERS TO ALL YOUR QUESTIONS LIE WITHIN YOU NOW, WAITING FOR YOU TO ASK FOR THEM.

Wonderful, you say. Sounds right. But how do I remember how to do it? Here's a condensed version.

Steps to Get Answers

1. Define the problem—what situation, relationship, or symptom is uppermost right now.
2. Meet with allies to get answers to: What's the message? Why? What should I do now?
3. If appropriate, resolve to consensus.
4. Act today and each day to carry out your allies' guidance. Be sure to check in each day for new instructions.
5. Share your newfound knowledge with someone it will serve.

We're here with you to the very end, or actually the new beginning. So, if you feel in your heart that now is the time for some change and this is a method that suits you, we are behind you 100 percent. Start by reading this book, getting Dr. Oyle's other books if you like, and finding support systems for yourself and your new life.

Decide this is what you want, feel the exhilaration, and the new ways will come into your life by the most wonderful and joyful "coincidences." Call us if you feel like it. We'd love to share in your journey to balance and wholeness.

Susan Jean and Dr. Irving Oyle are willing to assist you in applying the principles and methods described in this book. For more information, call:

> Dr. Irving Oyle   (503) 765-2663
> Susan Jean   (503) 765-4310

Through their Transformational Learning Center, they can also serve your small group or large organization by arranging a vacation retreat and seminar package on the Oregon coast. Each event is custom-tailored to the needs and desires of the participants. Call Susan Jean for details and arrangements.

COMPATIBLE BOOKS

FROM H J KRAMER INC

THE EARTH LIFE SERIES
by Sanaya Roman, Channel for Orin
A course in learning to live with joy,
sense energy, and grow spiritually.

LIVING WITH JOY, BOOK I
"I like this book because it describes the way I feel about
so many things."—VIRGINIA SATIR

PERSONAL POWER THROUGH AWARENESS:
A GUIDEBOOK FOR SENSITIVE PEOPLE, BOOK II
"Every sentence contains a pearl. . . ."—LILIAS FOLAN

SPIRITUAL GROWTH:
BEING YOUR HIGHER SELF, BOOK III
Orin teaches how to reach upward to align with the
higher energies of the universe, look inward to expand
awareness, and move outward in world service.

An Orin/DaBen Book
CREATING MONEY
by Sanaya Roman and Duane Packer, Ph.D.
This best-selling book teaches advanced manifesting techniques.

An Orin/DaBen Book
OPENING TO CHANNEL:
HOW TO CONNECT WITH YOUR GUIDE
by Sanaya Roman and Duane Packer, Ph.D.
This breakthrough book is the first
step-by-step guide to the art of channeling.

UNDERSTAND YOUR DREAMS
by Alice Anne Parker
A practical book that offers the reader
the key to dream interpretation.

THE COMPLETE HOME GUIDE TO AROMATHERAPY
by Erich Keller
An easy-to-use guide to aromatherapy that opens
the door to the magical world of natural scents.

WHEN FAIRY TALE ROMANCES BREAK REAL HEARTS
by Kimberley Heart
A guide to creating loving lasting relationships, using proven
methods for implementing real and sustainable life change.

YOU THE HEALER
by José Silva and Robert B. Stone
YOU THE HEALER is the complete course in Silva Method
techniques presented in a do-it-yourself forty-day format.

COMPATIBLE BOOKS

FROM H J KRAMER INC

WAY OF THE PEACEFUL WARRIOR
by Dan Millman
A tale of transformation and adventure . . . a worldwide best-seller.

SACRED JOURNEY OF THE PEACEFUL WARRIOR
by Dan Millman
The eagerly awaited sequel to the international best-selling
WAY OF THE PEACEFUL WARRIOR.

NO ORDINARY MOMENTS
by Dan Millman
*Based on the premise that we can change our world by
changing ourselves, this book shares an approach to life that turns
obstacles into opportunities, and experiences into wisdom.*

TALKING WITH NATURE
by Michael J. Roads
"From Australia comes a major new writer . . . a magnificent book!"
—RICHARD BACH, Author, *Jonathan Livingston Seagull*

JOURNEY INTO NATURE: A SPIRITUAL ADVENTURE
by Michael J. Roads
"If you only read one book this year, make that book
JOURNEY INTO NATURE."—*FRIEND'S REVIEW*

SIMPLE IS POWERFUL
by Michael J. Roads
*Embarking on a search for meaning and freedom in their lives, Michael
and Treenie discover that answers are often deceptively simple.*

IN SEARCH OF BALANCE
by John Robbins and Ann Mortifee
*An inquiry into issues and concerns of the heart from the
best-selling author of* DIET FOR A NEW AMERICA.

MESSENGERS OF LIGHT:
THE ANGELS' GUIDE TO SPIRITUAL GROWTH
by Terry Lynn Taylor
*At last, a practical way to connect with the
angels and to bring heaven into your life!*

GUARDIANS OF HOPE:
THE ANGELS' GUIDE TO PERSONAL GROWTH
by Terry Lynn Taylor
GUARDIANS OF HOPE *brings the angels down to earth
with over sixty practical angel practices.*

THE PERSECUTION AND TRIAL OF GASTON NAESSENS
by Christopher Bird
*The true story of the efforts to suppress an alternative treatment
for cancer, AIDS, and other immunologically based diseases.*